ED PODESTA
PAM CANNING

ITALIAN UNIFICATION 1815–1871

HODDER
EDUCATION
AN HACHETTE UK COMPANY

Acknowledgements

The authors and publisher would like to thank Christopher Duggan for his advice and expertise.

Dedication

To Marc for his endless patience and support. To Sarah, Maddy and Iris, for their patience and support. Also to Anna Pendry, a great teacher who set me on the right road.

Photo credits

p.2 © Hulton Archive/Getty; **p.9** © 2015 Photo Scala, Florence; **p.13** © DeAgostini/Getty Images; **p.16** © DeAgostini/Getty Images; **p.28** © DeAgostini/Getty Images; **p.34 & p.38** © Realy Easy Star/Alamy; **p.36** © Leemage/UIG via Getty Images; **p.39** © DEA/A. De Gregorio/De Agostini/Getty Images; **p.41** © MARKA/Alamy; **p.43** © The Gallery Collection/Corbis; **p.54** © Adolphe Braun & C; Francesco De Federicis/Alinari Archives, Florence/Alinari via Getty Images; **p.55** © Walker Art Library/Alamy; **p.56** *t* © Fine Art Images/Heritage Images/Getty Images; *b* Germania, 1848 (oil on canvas), Veit, Philipp (1793-1877)/© Germanisches Nationalmuseum, Nuremberg (Nuernberg), Germany/Bridgeman Images; **p.57** © DeAgostini/Getty Images; **p.66** © Illustrated London News Ltd/Mary Evans Picture Library; **p.69** © Leemage/UIG via Getty Images; **p.74 & 75** © The Print Collector/Heritage-Images/Getty Images; **p.79** © DEA Picture Library/Getty Images; **p.82** © MARKA/Alamy; **p.83** © Hulton Archive/Getty Images; **p.86** © Dea/G. Dagli Orti/De Agostini/Getty Images; **p.87** © Elio Ciol/Corbis; **p.91** © The Print Collector/Heritage-Images/Getty Images; **p.98** From Œuvres de Frédéric le Grand, Bd. 29, Berlin 1859 © University Library Trier (Digital Library); **p.102** © DEA/G. Dagli Orti/Getty Images; **p.103** © CuboImages srl/Alamy; **p.104** © Iugris/Alamy; **p.107** © Mary Evans Picture Library/Alamy; **p.118** © World History Archive/Alamy; **p.119** © Cambridge University Press; **p.120** © Penguin Press; © Cambridge University Press; **p.121** *t* © Fondazione Corriere della Sera, Archivo storico, *b* © Mondadori Portfolio via Getty Images; **p.122** © The Art Archive/Alamy; **p.123** © INTERFOTO/Alamy; **p.126** © Ann Ronan Picture Library/Heritage Images/Getty Images; **p.128** © Mary Evans Picture Library/Douglas Mccarthy; **p.134** © samott – Fotolia; **p.135** *t* © Chard (1964) Ltd, *b* © Realy Easy Star/Alamy.

Text credits

p.2 The Times, 19 April 1864; The Scotsman, 19 April 1864; **pp.10, 71** G.M. Trevelyan: from Garibaldi's Defence of the Roman Republic (Longmans, Green, and Co. 1907); **p.16** S.J. Woolf: from A History of Italy 1700–1860 (Routledge, 1991); **pp.28, 71** Lucy Riall: from Risorgimento (Palgrave Macmillan London, 2009); **p.34** Giuseppi Mazzini; **p.36** William Wordsworth, 'The Prelude' (1799); **p.39** Michael Morrogh: from The Unification of Italy (Documents & Debates) (Palgrave Macmillan, 2002); **p.41** Vincenzo Gioberti: from Del primate morale e civile degli italiani (1843); **p.43** C Duggan: from The Force of Destiny (Allen Lane, London, 2007); **p.50** Helge Berger and Mark Spoerer: from 'Economic Crises and the European Revolutions of 1848' from The Journal of Economic History, Vol. 61, No. 2, (June 2001); **p.61, 62, 128, 131** Denis Mack Smith: from The Making of Italy 1976–1870 (Harper and Row London, 1968); **p.71** Stuart Woolf: from A History of Italy 1700-1860. The Social Constraints of Political Change (London, 1979);

p.92 Martin Collier: from The Unification of Italy 1815–1870 (Heinemann, 2008); **p.94** R.F. Trager: from Long-term Consequences of Aggressive Diplomacy: European Relations after Austrian Crimean War Threats (Security Studies 21:232–265, 2012); **p.96** Orlando Figes: from Crimea (Penguin, London, 2010); **p.100** Edgar Feuchtwanger: from Imperial Germany 1850–1919 (London Routledge, 2001); **p.104** adapted from The Times, 7 June 1861; **p.108** Denis Mack Smith: from Cavour (Methuen, 1985); **p.116** The Spectator, 1 December 1855.

Orders: please contact Bookpoint Ltd, 130 Milton Park, Abingdon, Oxon OX14 4SB. Telephone: +44 (0)1235 827720. Fax: +44 (0)1235 400454. Lines are open 9.00a.m.– 5.00p.m., Monday to Saturday, with a 24-hour message answering service. Visit our website at www. hoddereducation.co.uk

© Ed Podesta, Pam Canning 2015
First published in 2015 by
Hodder Education,
An Hachette UK Company
338 Euston Road
London NW1 3BH

Impression number   10 9 8 7 6 5 4 3 2 1

Year   2019 2018 2017 2016 2015

Illustrations by Barking Dog Art
Typeset in 10pt Usherwood Book by DC Graphic Design Limited, Swanley Village, Kent
Printed in Italy

A catalogue record for this title is available from the British Library

ISBN 9781444178746

Contents

1 Italian unification: The essentials

Why did 600,000 British people flock to see a guerrilla fighter in 1864?

GARIBALDI IN ENGLAND: ARRIVAL OF GARIBALDI AT THE TOWNHALL, BARGATE, SOUTHAMPTON.—SEE PAGE 371.

△ Thousands of ordinary people flocked to see Garibaldi on his visit to England in 1864. This picture, published in the *London Illustrated News* in 1864, shows his entry into Southampton. His popularity was said to have irritated Queen Victoria who did not draw such large crowds.

In the summer of 1864 a veteran of several wars in South America and Italy visited England. This veteran, Giuseppe Garibaldi, was welcomed as a hero at the Crystal Palace in London by 'a multitude vaster than any with which those great halls are familiar' according to *The Times*, 19 April 1864. *The Scotsman* newspaper tells us that 'Women, more or less in full dress, flew upon him, seized his hands, touched his beard, his poncho, his trousers, any part of him that they could reach. […] They were delirious with excitement and behaved in [a] barbaric manner'.

This is the sort of reception a celebrity might receive today. Garibaldi was known as a brave fighter and a tactical genius, but this doesn't explain why he was given such a hero's welcome.

Ordinary people in mid-Victorian Britain had a passionate interest in what we call 'foreign affairs' – events abroad and the rivalries between countries. The British public had a great distrust of foreign autocratic empires, and often supported national groups who attempted to gain their freedom from such empires in order to become independent countries. In the view of many in Britain, Italy was one of these 'countries' fighting for independence, being dominated for most of the period from 1815 to 1860 by Austria. Garibaldi's exploits in leading the fight for Italian independence were seen by the British public as the latest part of the long story of the fight for freedom in the world.

Garibaldi's fame had begun in 1849 when he led the forces defending the radical Roman republic against the French army that had been sent to crush it. In the War of 1859 his leadership gave the Piedmontese Italians their only victory against the Austrians. Then in 1860 Garibaldi, with only a few thousand badly armed and untrained troops, conquered first Sicily and then the rest of the Kingdom of Naples and handed both of them over to the new King of Italy. This was a key moment in Italian history. Without Garibaldi, the new Kingdom might only have covered the north of the **peninsula**.

However, Garibaldi was popular in Britain not just because of his fight against the Austrians but also because his struggle for Italian unity and independence brought him into conflict with the Pope. In Britain there had been a long tradition of Anti-Papal feeling since the **Reformation** and Garibaldi was a potent symbol of brave resistance to the power not only of the Austrian Empire but to the Pope in Rome.

Garibaldi's image was also carefully stage managed by radical Italians who used Garibaldi's reputation as a man of action and moral virtue to inspire others to demand Italian unity. From Garibaldi's reception in Britain in 1864 it would seem that this PR campaign had worked.

peninsula
An area of land that is surrounded by water on three sides, but still joined to a mainland. Spain/Portugal and Italy are both very large peninsulas

Reformation
The process of protest and reform in the Catholic Church which began in the early 1500s and eventually saw the Church in Europe split between Protestant and Catholic faiths

Italian unification: an outline, 1796–1840

> **▪ Summarise** the story of Italian unification for those thinking of opting for it as an A level history course. Can you write it in 150 words?

What was the pattern of Italian unification? Was the process a step by step story of inevitable unification or was unification one of several possible outcomes? Pages 4–7 give you an outline, an idea of how likely Italian unification was from 1796 and introduces events and important personalities.

> The states of Italy can be referred to in different ways. The kingdom of Piedmont was officially called Piedmont-Sardinia because it was a union of the Duchy of Piedmont and the Kingdom of Sardinia. The Kingdom of Naples is often referred to as Naples and Sicily for similar reasons, but is also called The Kingdom of the Two Sicilies, for reasons too complex to explain here!

French dominance 1796–1815

Napoleon Bonaparte (1769–1821) became Emperor of France in 1804 due to his military and political skills. His empire dominated Western Europe, including Italy, until an alliance of countries defeated him in 1815.

Prince Metternich (1773–1859) was the leading Austrian politician and a key figure in European diplomacy. He had great influence over Austrian foreign policy, helping to maintain the balance of power in Europe (see page 16) until his resignation in 1848.

Revolts of 1820 and 1821

The people of Sicily revolted against rule from Naples in 1820. Next year in Piedmont army officers rebelled, hoping to force the Austrians out of Lombardy and Venetia. Both rebellions were put down by the Austrian army.

Restoration of 1815

Before 1815 Italy had been dominated by France but the 1815 Congress of Vienna gave Austria dominance over the Italian peninsula. Many rulers of the Italian states were restored to their positions before 1789. Austria's power prevented any change to this settlement until the late 1850s.

How likely was Italian unification?

| 1796 | 1800 | 1805 | 1810 | 1815 |

Essentials up to 1848

1. Italy was divided into different states before and after the defeat of Napoleon in 1815.

2. The peace settlement of 1815 gave Austria dominance over the Italian peninsula.

3. Some people wanted to see Italy get her independence from Austria, but few saw the need for unification.

4. Austria's power meant that the attempts to bring change to Italy met with failure.

Austrian dominance 1815–55

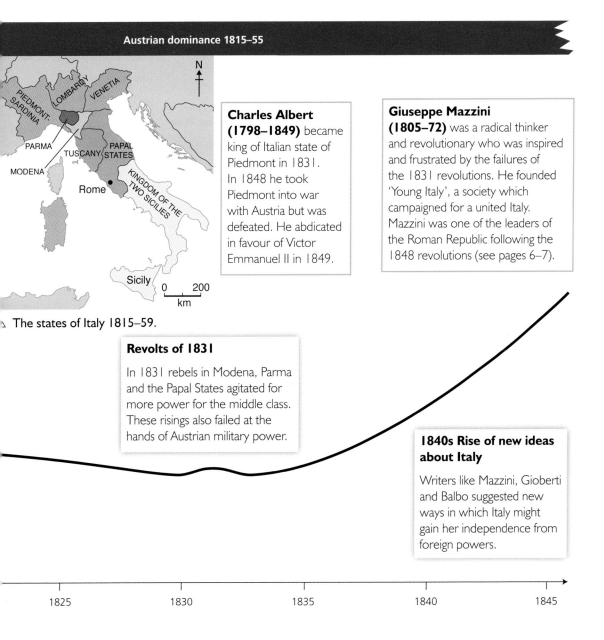

The states of Italy 1815–59.

Charles Albert (1798–1849) became king of Italian state of Piedmont in 1831. In 1848 he took Piedmont into war with Austria but was defeated. He abdicated in favour of Victor Emmanuel II in 1849.

Giuseppe Mazzini (1805–72) was a radical thinker and revolutionary who was inspired and frustrated by the failures of the 1831 revolutions. He founded 'Young Italy', a society which campaigned for a united Italy. Mazzini was one of the leaders of the Roman Republic following the 1848 revolutions (see pages 6–7).

Revolts of 1831

In 1831 rebels in Modena, Parma and the Papal States agitated for more power for the middle class. These risings also failed at the hands of Austrian military power.

1840s Rise of new ideas about Italy

Writers like Mazzini, Gioberti and Balbo suggested new ways in which Italy might gain her independence from foreign powers.

1825　　1830　　1835　　1840　　1845

Italian unification: an outline, 1848–70

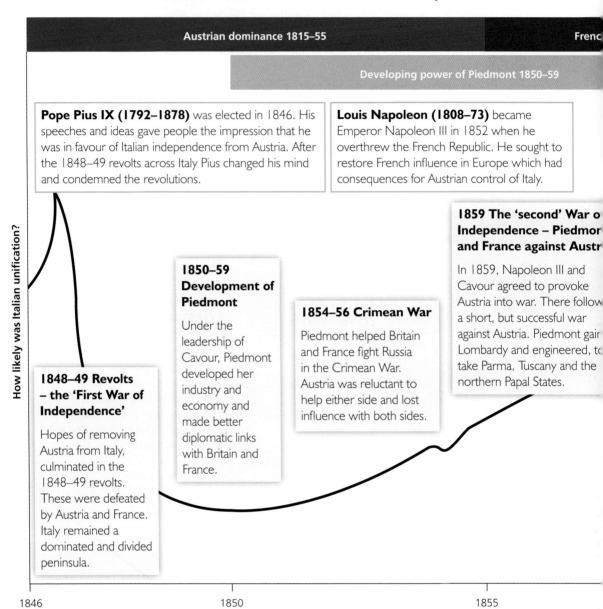

Austrian dominance 1815–55

Frenc

Developing power of Piedmont 1850–59

Pope Pius IX (1792–1878) was elected in 1846. His speeches and ideas gave people the impression that he was in favour of Italian independence from Austria. After the 1848–49 revolts across Italy Pius changed his mind and condemned the revolutions.

Louis Napoleon (1808–73) became Emperor Napoleon III in 1852 when he overthrew the French Republic. He sought to restore French influence in Europe which had consequences for Austrian control of Italy.

1859 The 'second' War o Independence – Piedmor and France against Austr

In 1859, Napoleon III and Cavour agreed to provoke Austria into war. There follow a short, but successful war against Austria. Piedmont gair Lombardy and engineered, to take Parma, Tuscany and the northern Papal States.

1850–59 Development of Piedmont

Under the leadership of Cavour, Piedmont developed her industry and economy and made better diplomatic links with Britain and France.

1854–56 Crimean War

Piedmont helped Britain and France fight Russia in the Crimean War. Austria was reluctant to help either side and lost influence with both sides.

1848–49 Revolts – the 'First War of Independence'

Hopes of removing Austria from Italy, culminated in the 1848–49 revolts. These were defeated by Austria and France. Italy remained a dominated and divided peninsula.

How likely was Italian unification?

1846   1850   1855

Unification and resistance 1861–70

In 1849 **Victor Emmanuel II (1820–78)** became king of Piedmont. He became a figure-head behind whom radicals and liberals could unite. In 1861 he was declared king of Italy following Garibaldi's southern campaign.

Count Camillo Benso of **Cavour (1810–61)** was Prime Minister of Piedmont during the 1850s. He led the economic and diplomatic development of Piedmont which led the way to unification.

Giuseppe **Garibaldi's (1807–82)** brave and charismatic command of the defence of the Roman Republic (see Chapter 8), made him a hero of unification. In 1860 he led a volunteer force to conquer the Kingdom of Naples for the newly formed Kingdom of Italy.

1860–70 The Brigands' War

A period of rebellion by southern peasants against rule from Piedmont.

1862 and 1867 Garibaldi's attempts to take Rome

Garibaldi made two more attempts to conquer Rome for the new Kingdom of Italy, risking war with France whose troops guarded the Pope.

1866 – Austro–Prussian War

The Kingdom of Italy allied with Prussia. Austria–Italian forces fared very badly. Despite this Italy gained Venetia.

1870 – Franco–Prussian War

In 1870 France was defeated by Prussia. The withdrawal of French troops from Rome allowed Italy to take Rome. Italy now had Rome as her capital, completing unification.

1860 – Garibaldi's campaign in the south

In a spectacular military campaign Garibaldi drove the forces of Naples from Sicily with only around a thousand volunteers. Next he toppled the King of Naples from his throne. Garibaldi handed over all his conquests to the King of Piedmont in 1861.

1860   1865   1870

Essentials 1848–70

1. Despite large scale revolts like those in 1848–49 Austria's position in Italy seemed very strong.

2. Piedmont's development in the 1850s made her the 'leading state' of Italy, and attracted liberals and radicals.

3. The Crimean War created new alliances and isolated Austria

4. Napoleon, Cavour and Garibaldi all took opportunities to change the situation. Unification took place in several stages.

5. When Italy was unified, many 'Italians' resisted control from Piedmont.

National myths and teleology: Was Italy destined to be united?

An important focus of this book is the idea of 'nation' – of country or nationhood. What makes a nation a nation? Understanding this will help you assess the extent of the problem faced by those who wanted to build a new 'Italian' nation.

By thinking carefully about the processes that encouraged and resisted the unification of Great Britain as a country, we hope that you will see that countries are not 'given', but created by people thinking and acting in circumstances and within processes that sometimes they cannot control. The creation of such countries was therefore not inevitable.

The Bonny Bunch of Roses, a traditional British folk song from just after the end of the Napoleonic Wars celebrates the unity of Britain:

> O, son, be not too venturesome;
>
> For England has a heart of oak;
>
> And England, Ireland, and Scotland,
>
> The unity has never been broke.

The song suggests that British unity was timeless, endless and perhaps even a natural state of affairs. However, Britain's unity was created over many centuries, much longer than the time in which some hoped to achieve Italian unity. Wales was united forcibly with England through invasion, conquest and castle-building after the Norman Conquest in 1066, a process finished by Edward I whose reign ended in 1307. Unity between England and Scotland happened 400 years later. This time it was not war that created unity but a financial crisis. Scotland and England signed the Act of Union in 1707 partly to save Scotland from bankruptcy. In more recent centuries British unity has been strengthened by very different experiences. The expansion of Britain's empire gave English, Scots and Welsh soldiers and settlers a new arena in which to work together and to expand their sense of British-ness. Sharing resistance to common enemies during the French Revolution and the wars that followed in which Napoleon dominated Western Europe, created intense feelings of British nationalism in opposition to France. Historians such as David Reynolds argue that the World Wars of the twentieth century had the same effect.

Britain's present unity is built on England's identity as a successful democracy with a strong culture and constitutional roots that stretch back into the Saxon period. This includes shared ideas about how a country should be run, and trust in institutions such as the monarchy, the police and parliament.

Therefore unity in Britain came about partly through military force, partly through chance and economic factors, and partly because threats from abroad brought the countries within Britain closer together. This unity was strengthened and is maintained by a shared political culture of democracy.

However, this process was not a one-way street. The creation of a United Kingdom was completed despite armed opposition, and political and cultural resistance in Ireland, Wales and Scotland. Political and cultural barriers also persisted long after each country was taken over by the English and culture became part of the battle for domination. The fact of cultural difference was one weapon used by the English in their domination of the other 'nations' of the British Isles. We can find countless references in historical sources to the superiority of English culture and fierce criticism of 'inferior' and 'uncivilised' Irish, Welsh and Scottish culture. However, the experience of domination often led to a self-conscious revival of local culture. The Welsh language, culture and sense of difference from their English over-lords became deliberately celebrated. This cultural independence has continued in Wales until the present, especially since the 1970s when Welsh language education and street signs were put up, and paid for, by the British state. Cultural differences have often spilled over into conflict and sometimes terrorism. The revival of interest in Irish literary culture, history and language in the late nineteenth century was followed in the early twentieth by the 1916 Easter Rising. Violence continued throughout: independence, civil war and then in the terrorism seen in Northern Ireland from the 1960s until the late 1990s.

Just recently more peaceful, democratic but powerful tensions and forces challenge the links uniting the country. In September 2014 there was a referendum on whether Scotland should leave the Union and become an independent state. Although the result was clear, it was close. The effect of the vote on the way that Britain is governed in the future remains uncertain.

△ This poster, made between 1870 and 1914, shows the great men and the people of Italy working together to complete unification of Italy with '*Italia Irredenta*', the parts of nearby countries which Italy claimed should be Italian.

History and nationhood

There has often been a really important connection between writing about the history of a country and the process of nation-building. During the nineteenth century, historians in Britain were part of the process of building British national feeling. This writing focused on the development of liberty, the growth of the power of Parliament and the creation of an

Empire that, it was argued, brought civilisation to primitive people across the globe.

Other countries also developed their own national stories. This was especially true of new countries like Italy where it was hoped that history could play its part in uniting the different parts of the peninsula. Therefore, in the first writings about the period 1800 to 1870, Italian historians in the late 1800s emphasised the idea of **Risorgimento** or the re-birth of the Italian spirit. They saw this new Italy as a break from the weakness, divisions and foreign domination of Italy in past centuries. Instead the new Italy of 1870 was inheriting the glorious distant pasts of the Romans and the Renaissance.

Risorgimento
The idea of a 're-birth' of the Italian spirit and nation

These early histories also focused particularly on the deeds of 'great men' such as Cavour, Garibaldi, Mazzini and Victor Emmanuel, all working together in a perfect blend to help Italy reach her 'inevitable' destiny – unification. It was hoped that Italians reading this heroic history of the *Risorgimento* would discover a sense of patriotism and collective endeavour, and through hard work and collaboration between all classes and regions, make Italy a strong nation in the world.

Historians call this kind of story a 'teleological' story, one where the writing shows an inevitable path or destiny to a country's history. Italian historians were echoed in this by writers from England such as **G. M. Trevelyan** who celebrated the *Risorgimento* as a glorious episode in Italian history, not least because it led to the formation of a liberal state with parliamentary government along very similar lines to the British state. The heroic deeds of the great men were presented in such a way as to foster feelings of patriotism and admiration. Here is a great example from Trevelyan's *Garibaldi's Defence of The Roman Republic* which was published in 1907.

G. M. Trevelyan was a talented and popular historian writing in the early twentieth century. His writing celebrated liberal ideas of freedom and constitutional government.

> There was needed, too, a warrior hero of a new type, rival to the figures of Charlemagne and the crusaders who should win the heart by firing the imagination of Europe. [...] Garibaldi had now won Italy's devotion, and was helping to unite her divided children by their common pride in himself. Ere long he was to dazzle the imagination of Europe.

Trevelyan's books were designed for a popular audience and the same tone can been seen in the public lectures given by the historian J. A. R. Marriott in 1889. In one lecture, he said: 'It is my purpose to speak of the work of the great men of action, of Mazzini, of Cavour, of Garibaldi.'

However, Marriott saved his most effusive praise for Victor Emanuel II of Italy, saying that he was also going to write about 'him whose coolness and courage, whose temperate zeal and whose unswerving honesty, whose clearness of vision and unfailing common sense gave consistency and coherence to the lifework of them all. I speak of course of Victor Emmanuel'. We must be careful not to take Marriott's description as the unvarnished truth. Indeed this is quite a romantic and idealised description of the first King of Italy. We learn from other sources that the new king sulked his way around a forced tour of his new Kingdom after 1861, during which he told (in French), an Italian peasant who kneeled before him, that he wanted to 'kick [him] up the arse'!

Since the late nineteenth century, historians have continued to reinterpret and research the process through which the individual states of the Italian peninsula became unified. These reinterpretations have challenged the idea that unification was predestined, suggesting that the outcome of events could have been very different. This book will help you examine and understand these different interpretations and will also ask you to look beyond the historical headlines, to question the stories of glory and bravery that you will sometimes be presented with. Later on we will return to this theme of historiography, but in the meantime we want you to remember the image of a sulky king fantasising about kicking a peasant. Bring this picture to mind when the story of unification seems to be too perfect, or the bravery of the participants seems to be exaggerated.

Why should we study the unification of Italy?

This is an excellent period for A level studies because you need to question 'everyday' concepts that at first sight seem self-evident or obvious. For instance, you will be asking 'what is a nation?' and 'does history have an underlying story or direction?' You will use original sources, not just as a record of what happened, but so that you can understand the ideas, motives and fears of those who were present at and active in the events of unification.

Studying Italian unification is also a window into an important time in European history, and helps you to understand how the nationalism of that period has shaped, for good and ill, the political landscape and history of Europe in recent times. Italy became unified at the same time as Germany. This was also at the same time as Austria's position weakened in central Europe to which Austria tried to respond by turning attention eastwards towards the crumbling Ottoman Empire. These events and shifting alliances eventually saw the rise of tension between Russia, Austria and the Slavic peoples of the Balkans, culminating in the assassination of Archduke Franz Ferdinand in 1914 and the start of the First World War. None of these events were inevitable but they all had their roots in the period that you are about to study.

In studying Italy we should also be aware that we need to learn how such a divided and diverse peninsula came to have one government, and that such countries and governments are made by people, rather than given or created by history. Understanding its past will help us read the news about Italy – her economic problems, corruption at high levels of government, divisions between northern and southern provinces, and political parties that wish to split the country in two.

Comprehending its history will make us aware that Italy's past does much to explain Italy's current debates and problems. It is even possible that the process of unification has not finished and that the continued existence of one, united country of Italy is not guaranteed.

Napoleon's Europe, 1792–1815

Key:
— France in 1812
— France in 1792
☐ Satellite states

△ France before and during the Napoleonic Era. As you can see from this map, Napoleon's ambition was great, and the height of his power reflected the reach of his ambition.

Europe under Napoleon, 1812

Napoleon was the French hero of the wars between revolutionary France and the other powers of Europe following the French Revolution that began in 1789. Napoleon conquered Italy after invasions in 1796 and 1800 and eventually seized the French throne, becoming Emperor of France in 1804. Napoleon's military skills and the military power of France meant that by 1812 France dominated Western Europe. Austria, Prussia, Russia and Britain remained independent countries but all, apart from Britain, had at one point been defeated by Napoleon's forces and been forced to agree peace terms with Napoleon.

The Revolutionary (1792–1802) and Napoleonic Wars (1803–15)

After the start of the French Revolution in 1789 the other European powers grew increasingly worried about the possibility of the spread of revolutionary ideas. From 1792, different coalitions of European powers declared war on France, in attempts to restore the French monarchy. Though there were brief periods of peace, the fighting continued as Napoleon's power grew and France shifted from a war of defence to a war of conquest. As the map shows, by 1812 Napoleon had built up a substantial empire, creating satellite states which he hoped would ensure that France continued to dominate the continent.

The ideals of the French Revolution

The revolution in France saw the destruction of what is known as 'the *ancien Regime*' a term historians use to describe the traditional monarchies and aristocracies that ruled Europe in the eighteenth century and before. The revolution tore down this *ancien regime* and in its place raised a new order of 'nations' and 'rationalism'. Napoleon then exported these ideas to Europe. It was hoped that loyalty to one's national group instead of a monarch or ruler, the creation of new 'rational' laws and the re-drawing of boundaries and development of government would lead to a new Europe under French guidance and leadership in which there would be peace and prosperity.

◁ This grand painting disguises Napoleon's humble beginnings on the Island of Corsica, but it vividly shows his ambition for power, and the self-confidence which helped him to conquer most of Western Europe in the years 1796–1815.

The defeat of Napoleon, 1815

In 1812 Napoleon decided to punish Russia for her refusal to stop trading with France's leading enemy – Britain. However, Napoleon's invasion of Russia proved to be a disaster. Napoleon had hoped for a decisive victory but the Russians refused to be drawn into battle. Instead they withdrew further and further into Russia, forcing Napoleon to continue further from his territory and into the depths of winter, causing terrible losses and the eventual destruction of Napoleon's *Grande Armée*, the Imperial Army which he had hoped would conquer Russia. The remains of his army were chased to the borders of France by Russia and later by a coalition of Prussia, Britain, Russia and Austria. In 1815 the representatives of the coalition met in Vienna to decide to what extent the borders, rulers and other power structures of Europe's *ancien regime* should be 'restored' after Napoleon's defeat. After a brief attempt to regain power in that same year, Napoleon was defeated for the final time at the Battle of Waterloo. The Treaty of Paris in November 1815 confirmed most of the Treaty of Vienna, but imposed much harsher restrictions on France than the earlier treaty.

Insight

13

Napoleon's Italy

Milan

Venice

KINGDOM OF ITALY

Genoa

Rome

Naples

KINGDOM OF NAPLES

KINGDOM OF SARDINIA

KINGDOM OF SICILY

N

Key:

French Empire

Under French control

0   200
km

△ Italy, though still divided, was re-organised and re-divided under Napoleon. Only parts of Italy were taken into the French Empire, the rest of Italy became two separate 'satellite' states.

Who ruled Italy during the French occupation?

If you compare the map on page 14 with the one on page 5, you can see that the Papal States and Piedmont were part of the French Empire until 1815. This meant that they were ruled by Paris directly. The Kingdom of Italy itself was restricted to the north of the peninsula, and was really a puppet state of France. Important positions were given to Napoleon's friends and relations. Napoleon himself was 'King of Italy', but it was ruled by his step-son. The Kingdom of Naples was ruled by his brother-in-law, Joachim Murat. Napoleon's son, François was given the decorative title of King of Rome.

Did the French Unite Italy?

Although Napoleon ran an empire, and not a **republic**, the places he conquered were re-organised under modern, progressive ideals. For instance, the French system of civil laws, the 'code Napoleon', was imposed including modern ideas such as divorce by agreement. **Feudal rights** were abolished across the territories that Napoleon conquered. Duchies, Kingdoms and Papal rule across northern Italy were brought to an end. **Tariffs** (internal customs taxes) that prevented trade between the different states were also abolished, and new roads and telegraph lines were built.

While the Church lost power and influence, many of the urban middle classes (lawyers, bankers, merchants) did very well. They worked in the governments installed by the French, and purchased much of the land confiscated from the Church, often at a cheap price. Businesses in general did well – they found it easier to buy and sell goods across Italy because of the new roads, and the ending of tariffs. In 1796, Napoleon launched an essay competition in Milan, to encourage writers to suggest the best way of ruling Italy. It could therefore be argued that French rule encouraged the idea of a single nation of Italy through: the imposition of similar laws across the peninsula; improved communication and transportation between the different areas and the removal of trade barriers as well as joining some states into larger kingdoms.

However, as the Napoleonic period went on, many people grew increasingly resentful of French rule. French conscription of Italian men to fight and die for the French Empire was hated by many Italians. In 1812, 27,000 Italian soldiers took part in Napoleon's invasion of Russia but only 1000 badly wounded or very sick soldiers returned. Italians also hated the high taxes placed on Italy to pay for these wars – 60 per cent of the tax raised in Italy was spent on the military.

Resentment led some people, encouraged by the Catholic Church, to take part in revolts and riots against rule from Paris. However, few of those who wanted to resist Napoleon's rule wanted to replace it with a united Italy. They wanted the restoration of their own local dukes and kings. They would have seen rule by another 'Italian' as being just as foreign as French rule.

republic
This is a state which is ruled by a 'president', rather than a monarch. Republics are often democratic, where voters choose the president

feudal rights
Traditional rights enjoyed by landlords over peasants. They varied from place to place but often involved taxes on the use of mills for grinding grain or using roads or bridges

tariffs
Taxes levied on goods imported into a state. These taxes made goods from other parts of Italy more expensive than local goods and so hampered trade between the different states

Insight

2 Why was Italian unification so unlikely before 1848?

△ Prince Klemens von Metternich (1773–1859) was the Foreign Minister of the Austrian Empire from 1809 to 1848 and the Austrian Emperor's chief minister from 1821 to 1848. Metternich was one of the most powerful and influential politicians of the period covered by this book. Many historians credit him with deciding the overall direction and design of the 1815 peace settlement following the defeat of Napoleonic France.

'Italian affairs do not exist.' Metternich 1815

'Italy is merely a geographical expression.' Metternich 1847

'For Metternich, the Italian peninsula, […] represented a passive object of European diplomacy: […] Italy's importance lay in its territorial divisions, essential for the maintenance of the balance of power.'
S. J. Woolf, A History of Italy 1700–1860 (1986)

These three quotations, two from the leading European statesman at the negotiations at Vienna in 1815 and one from a historian, show us that Italy was expected to remain divided in the years following the defeat of Napoleon. Italy's divisions were seen by the major European powers as vitally important in maintaining the '**balance of power**' between those nations, particularly in ensuring that France could not again threaten Europe by dominating Italy and then using Italy's resources to help expand her borders elsewhere in Europe. To achieve this the great powers insisted that the thrones and titles of the different Italian states, their armies, trades, taxes and resources should be split up amid the different Italian states, and Austria given the job of guarding them. In this way France would have to befriend each state, or defeat each state, in the face of Austrian opposition, if she were to increase her power and influence in Italy.

The '**balance of power**' was an idea that peace could be maintained by ensuring that no country was so powerful that it could dominate the others in Europe. The idea meant different things to each government. In Austria, it meant that France should not become a threat to peace in the way that she was before 1815. Britain was concerned that Russia did not become too powerful, whereas in France, especially after 1848, it was felt that Austria had too much power and that France should be allowed to increase her influence on the continent.

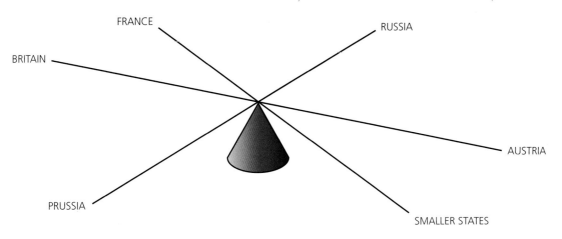

FRANCE

RUSSIA

BRITAIN

AUSTRIA

PRUSSIA

SMALLER STATES

△ There was never a perfect balance between the different powers, mainly because their relations changed as the period went on. The idea was that maintaining a balance as much as possible would help avoid another destructive period of war like the Napoleonic Wars.

However, there is a subtle difference in the tone of the two quotations from Metternich. The first, from 1815, shows Metternich confident that Italy would play the part assigned to her in these plans. At that time Metternich was certain that Italy would not be making its way towards any form of political self-awareness, and none of the **Great Powers** had any intention that Italy should be formed into one country. The second quotation, from 1847, sounds just as determined but we might think its tone is too shrill, too stridently dismissive, perhaps reflecting Metternich's anxiety that the growth of the idea of the Italian nation in the minds of some thinkers might now be threatening the balance of power that Metternich had helped to construct 30 years earlier at the Vienna peace conference.

Why did Metternich feel so confident after 1815, when he said 'Italian affairs do not exist'? This chapter will help you to understand what lay behind this confidence and why Italian unity was so unlikely before 1848. However, a word of warning is necessary here. It is easy to assume that Metternich was wrong in 1815, that Italian unification was bound to happen because it did eventually happen. We do not agree that this was the case. There were very powerful forces working against unification. So we have tried to be careful about our language as we write this and later chapters, as sometimes writers on Italian unification have made it seem as if the process of unification was inevitable, that Italian history was always working towards the point of unity in 1860. This chapter is therefore designed to help you understand why Italian unity was so unlikely in the years between 1815 and 1848, not what was 'preventing' or 'holding back' Italy from taking her place among the nations.

Britain, France Russia and Austria, were often referred to as the **Great Powers** of Europe, as they were the most powerful countries at that time. As our period went on Prussia's power increased until she too could be described as one of the 'Great Powers'.

■ **Enquiry Focus:** Why was Italian unification so unlikely before 1848?

You will be studying six factors that explain why unification was so unlikely in the years before 1848:

Geographical divisions

The Vienna Settlement of 1815: Italy's role in the peace of Europe

Political and social differences between the Italian states

Differences in language and culture

Class divisions

The role of the Catholic Church

1 You will need six pieces of paper (perhaps three A4 sheets cut in half), or six large index cards. Write one factor heading at the top of each piece of paper.

2 Skim read each section of this chapter and then write a sentence at the top of each piece of paper. These sentences should be your first impression of the effect that each factor had on the potential for Italian unity.

3 Re-read each section, this time searching for and noting down evidence to back up your first impression. If necessary, also use this second reading to improve the sentence at the top of each piece of paper.

> Here we can see that this sentence has changed on the second reading of the chapter.

> This sentence is your explanation of how this factor helped to prevent unification.

> These bullet-point notes are the evidence that you will gather during the second reading of this chapter.

Geographical divisions

created barriers and differences and

Italy's geography made it hard to unite as one country *because the different parts of Italy were isolated from the others.*
- The Apennine Mountains divided east from west and north from south.
- There wasn't a lot of trade in goods or agriculture.
- The dry climate and poor soils of the south made peasants poorer than the peasants in the cooler and wetter north.
- Transportation was difficult - mountains, no navigable rivers, etc.

At the end of the chapter you will think about the relative impact of these factors, how they were interrelated, and whether one factor underpinned the lack of unity found in Italy before 1848. You will find further details on page 29.

Factor 1: Geographical divisions

Unification was made unlikely by the geography of Italy. As you can see from the map opposite, the length of the peninsula, the lack of navigable rivers upon which boats could travel, and the scale of the Apennine Mountains made travel very difficult between the different cities and centres of Italian trade. The Apennines have the effect not only of isolating west from east, but also north from south. It was easier to load goods onto a ship and sail them around the 'boot' of the peninsula than it was to take them by road over the Apennines from the east to the west coasts. The impact of the geographical features also meant it was not unusual for citizens and subjects of the states of northern Italy to see those from the south as foreigners. Northern Italians often felt they had much more in common with their French, Swiss and Austrian neighbours than they had with those living in the south.

Geographical differences also led to a divide in the basic agricultural economy of the peninsula. The Po valley in the north is the only large plain in the whole peninsula, and by the nineteenth century was the agricultural powerhouse of Italy, fuelling the prosperity of the north. This wealth contrasted with the poverty of the south where primitive farming methods and the lack of good soil and pasture for animals, all contributed to poverty and the inability of the land to feed the population. The historian Christopher Duggan describes a 'vicious spiral' in which deforestation, caused by people seeking to live higher and higher in the hills to avoid the floods and malaria caused by the run off of rain, in turn caused more flooding and malaria, which drove people to leave the plains and clear more areas of forest. These differences in living conditions were among the reasons why 'Italians' from the north looked down on the much poorer people from the south, and made unification between the prosperous and productive north and the poorer south much less attractive from the point of view of the northerners.

Another issue working against the idea of a single state was the localisation of agriculture. Most agricultural produce was consumed in the area where it was produced so there was little to sell elsewhere and therefore make a profit. In turn, this meant there was no incentive for farmers to invest in new production methods. In some cases peasants were even suspicious of ideas such as spreading manure in order to improve their soil. Duggan gives the example of some in Sicily being, as late as the 1950s, unwilling to do this in case it made the soil 'dirty'. New ideas did not spread very easily among peasants, a theme to which we will return, and there were few incentives for peasants to communicate with their neighbouring village, town or state or to consider these as places as a source of new ideas. These divisions meant that peasants were unlikely to see themselves as part of a larger 'Italian' identity.

■ If this is the first time you have read this section, jot down a sentence on your card headed 'Geographical divisions' to explain how the geography of Italy made unity unlikely. Then move on to read the next section.

If this is the second time you have read this chapter, take a look at the sentence you jotted down the first time. Do you still agree with what you wrote, or do you need to edit what you first thought? Once you are happy with your sentence, note down evidence in bullet points underneath it. Use this evidence to support your analysis of the effect of this factor.

Italian Alps

Po Plain

Milan

Venice

Turin

River Po

Florence

ELBA

River Tiber

Apennines

Rome

Adriatic Sea

Naples

SARDINIA

Tyrrhenian Sea

Palermo

Ionian Sea

SICILY

N

Mediterranean Sea

0   200
km

△ This map of Italy shows its geographical features – take careful note of how little of the country is flat, and the way that the mountains separate east from west and north from south.

Factor 2: The Vienna Settlement of 1815: Italy's role in the peace of Europe

Italy was a peninsula divided into a number of independent states. This division had existed since the end of Roman times (about 500AD) although the period of French occupation (1792–1815) had seen some changes – with fewer, larger states created by France. However, the older divisions of Italy were re-created in 1815 at the Vienna Congress by the countries that had defeated Napoleon. Their plan was that the peninsula was to play two roles, both of which worked against any idea of unification.

The first of these roles was to create a barrier to prevent French conquests in Europe by ensuring that Italy did not fall under French control again. To achieve this, the state of Piedmont-Sardinia was restored and given control over the Republic of Genoa. Piedmont was therefore restored to act as a strong **buffer state** against France, to prevent France invading Italy and using Italy's resources to threaten other European countries.

Italy's second role was to provide rewards for Austria. Austria had lost influence and territory in Germany but the Vienna settlement compensated for this by giving Austria substantial territory in and authority over large areas of the Italian peninsula. This rewarded Austria but also allowed it to use influence and power to prevent any future French attempts to gain influence in Italy.

Another decision at Vienna was to restore some of the ruling families who had been in charge before Napoleon's invasions. In Naples the Bourbon King Ferdinand was restored, as were Duke Ferdinand III in Tuscany, Victor Emmanuel I in Piedmont, and the Pope in the Papal States. However, apart from Piedmont, the restored states of Italy all lacked powerful armies and relied on Austrian guarantees and treaties to provide the military power needed to protect their states from revolution or invasion. Some states were not restored, such as the Republic of Genoa, which was annexed to Piedmont, and the Republic of Venice, which went to Austria as part of Lombardy-Venetia. So, while many duchies and all of the monarchies were restored in Italy, the republics were not, as these were deemed to be too unstable, and too open to political radicalism following the events of the wars of the French Republic and then the Napoleonic domination of Europe that followed.

This re-creation of a piecemeal Italy, the **restoration** of dukes and kings who would require the military help of Austria, and the direct control by Austria of Lombardy-Venetia therefore all worked against the unification of Italy.

Buffer states are states between two powerful states who take on a role (sometimes reluctantly) of acting as a way of preventing conflict between these states, or as a way of protecting a group of smaller states from a more powerful neighbour. Sometimes buffer states are meant to prevent a state from expanding. Piedmont seemed to be playing many of these roles after 1815.

restoration
Usually refers to the re-instatement of a monarch or ruler after a period of rebellion or revolution

---

▪ After the first time you read this section, jot down a sentence to explain how this factor prevented unity in Italy. When you have finished, move on to reading the next section.

When you have read this section a second time, take another look at your sentence of analysis. Do you still agree with it? If not, re-write the sentence before recording supporting evidence underneath in bullet point form.

Factor 3: Political and social differences between the Italian states

Before 1861 there was no kingdom of Italy. Until that day, Italy was divided into different states, some large, some small. This division was not the only thing that worked against unification between 1815 and 1848. The states had very different political, social and economic features that also made unification unlikely:

- Austrian influence over each of the states. Austria's strong interest in maintaining the status quo in Italy acted as a brake against any form of political change.

- Trade barriers. These prevented Italians from becoming wealthier and also prevented communication between the different states and between different classes.

- Educational differences. In some states the lack of literacy meant that new political ideas and movements could not be communicated to the majority of Italians living there. In other states the education system deliberately focused on science and engineering so that more troublesome subjects that might encourage revolution (such as politics and history) could be left off the syllabus.

- Attitudes to Napoleonic reforms and to change. Some of the restored rulers wanted to remove modernising changes introduced after the French invasion of 1792, while others embraced some changes the French had brought. This left Italy with a patchwork of different laws, but also with rulers who were suspicious of change and of modern ideas.

Austrian control

The Italian peninsula was dominated by Austria from 1815 until 1859 and Austria remained a barrier to the final unification of Italy until 1870. It was in Austria's interest to use this domination to keep Italy as a group of separate states. Not only did Austria get a large proportion of its total tax income from its Italian possessions, it was also in Austrian interests to prevent Italian nationalism more generally. Austria's empire was highly diverse as it ruled over Serbs, Croats, Poles, Germans, Hungarians and other nations. If Italian national feeling was allowed to develop and if Austria's Italian provinces gained their independence then this might threaten the stability of the rest of the Austrian Empire, where other nations might also be encouraged to protest or seek independence.

The Austrians exercised this control in several ways:

- They ruled Lombardy and Venetia directly, as provinces of the Austrian Empire.

- Close relatives of the Austrian Emperor ruled the duchies of Tuscany, Modena and Parma. This last state was ruled by the Emperor's daughter Marie Louise, who was also the widow of Napoleon.

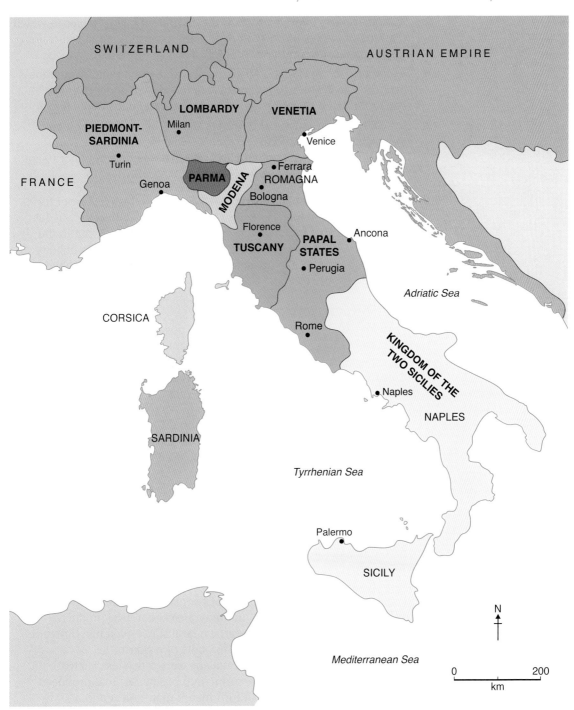

△ The Italian peninsula after the restoration in 1815.

- Austria also used devices such as the 1815 treaty with Naples in which the King of Naples promised not to grant a constitution in return for military assistance in the event of invasion or revolution.
- As a Catholic country, the Austrians also acted as a military guarantor over the Papal States – the Pope would need their support as the Papacy lacked a proper army of its own to defend the Papal States.
- In 1820, Austria, Russia and Prussia signed the Troppau Protocol in which they promised to use their powers to prevent revolt or revolution in Europe, another clear sign that Austria would not tolerate any effort to bring change to Italy.

In this way the influence of Austria acted as a very effective barrier for change in the years before 1848. As you will see, this influence was felt many times, not only in drawing up the settlement of 1815, but in the revolutions of 1820–21, 1831 and 1848–49 when the Austrian military played an important role in quashing revolts which threatened change in the peninsula.

Trade barriers

Renaissance
A period in the 1500s which saw a revival of art, literature, music and science. Italy's wealthy merchants spent huge sums on works of art and her trade with Muslim merchants brought new knowledge and culture. Italy was the crossroads of the Renaissance world

In the Middle Ages and **Renaissance** Italy's position in the middle of the Mediterranean had made her an important crossroads for trade and culture; a place where goods from Europe, Africa and the Middle East could be traded. However, by the eighteenth and nineteenth centuries, the focus of world trade had shifted to the Atlantic. For Italy this meant that, while the north of the peninsula continued to trade with the rest of Europe (especially in fine goods such as glassware and silk), the south of Italy became economically isolated from the north. In part this was due to the geography of Italy – as we have already seen the mountains created difficulties in trading across the peninsula.

However, there were other trade barriers too. The re-creation of the different states of Italy meant that each ruler had to raise money to run their state, to pay pensions to their ministers and favourites, make gifts, pay wages and run armies. One of the important ways in which the rulers could do this was through customs duties or tariffs. These were taxes on goods imported into each state from abroad or from other states. These tariffs therefore made trade between states less profitable. This lack of profit meant there was no incentive for people to trade between states. Tariffs weren't the only barrier – in many areas poor food production did not allow large surpluses to be grown, and states even had different methods of weighing or measuring amounts of products.

parochial
A very localised set of attitudes and experiences

These trade barriers meant that Italians were much less likely to develop their farming or manufacturing into businesses that produced large amounts of goods, which in turn meant that traders and businessmen didn't see the value of developing links between states and had fewer reasons to communicate with 'Italians' in other states. This added to the sense of **parochialism**, which we can see preventing change or any moves towards unification. For example, in 1831, the leaders of a revolt in Bologna refused to send soldiers or aid to another 'foreign' revolt in Modena.

Educational differences

There were large differences in the ways, and the extent to which the people of the states of Italy were educated. Lombardy and Venetia, which were part of the Austrian Empire, had a very high standard of education. Children in these areas were especially well educated in the sciences, as it was felt that studying history might awaken ideas of nationalism that might encourage radicalism and threaten Austria's rule. In contrast, education was very underdeveloped in Piedmont. Even when primary schooling was supposedly made compulsory after 1822, many children in Piedmont did not go to school.

In Naples and the Papal States education was made the responsibility of the Catholic Church. The Church was very suspicious of nationalism, which threatened the **temporal power** of the Papacy. The Church also regarded liberal calls for progress and freedom as selfish and egotistical, and used education, alongside their control of censorship of books in both states as a way of combatting the spread of such ideas. These differences, and the control of education by the Church, meant that education was basic where it took place at all, and even then was often focused on transmitting the values of the Church rather than on instilling a sense of national identity. In 1871, only around 31 per cent of the population of Italy could read. The fact that so few Italians could read meant that it was very difficult for those hoping to encourage ideas of nationalism and progress to communicate with or persuade the vast majority of the population. We can see this problem in the difficulties that **Mazzini** had in expanding his appeal beyond the literate middle classes in northern Italy after 1832.

Attitudes to Napoleonic reforms and to change

The period of French rule before 1815 was remembered by many rulers of the Italian states as a time of turbulence, change and destruction. After 1815 many of these rulers kept only one aspect of the reforms which the French had introduced – the tax system. They kept this French innovation because it was so successful. Most other changes introduced during the period of French domination were removed by the new regimes. For instance, in Piedmont Victor Emmanuel I set about literally ripping up the changes that the French had brought, including parks and streetlights (run by gas) that they had built. He brought back the feudal taxes and church privileges, dug up roads, cancelled the Code Napoleon (the civil and criminal laws set up by the French), discriminated against Jews and Protestants and sacked all those appointed to government jobs. In short, Victor Emanuel wanted things to be just like they were in 1796, before the French invaded.

The Papacy also did much to return the areas under its rule to the way things had been before the Napoleonic invasions. The laymen who had been given positions in the administration of these areas were removed from their posts and **cardinals** and priests were re-established as administrators. However, in Tuscany Duke Ferdinand III, the brother of the Austrian Emperor, was a modernising ruler. He kept many of the changes that had been brought in by Napoleon, including the code of laws. Some officials were even allowed to keep their positions.

temporal power
Real, worldly power and authority as a sovereign or government

Mazzini was a radical Italian nationalist who was convinced that the best way for Italy to unite would be through a revolution of ordinary Italians across the peninsula (see Chapter 3 for more about Mazzini).

cardinal
An important office in the Catholic Church. Cardinals have an important role in electing a new Pope, and in running the Catholic Church. At the time of this study they also had important jobs as administrators in the government of the Papal States

This meant that Italy was not a unified country waiting to happen, but a diverse set of legal and administrative systems, each with different groups who either wanted to bring change or maintain the status quo. In some areas there were groups who had been excluded from power (the middle-class administrators who were removed from positions of power in the Papal Legations, for instance) and who would prove to be difficult for the restored regimes. However, even these groups didn't foresee or actively struggle for the unification of the whole peninsula. They were concerned with regaining power in their own states, and often in their own cities or parishes.

> ■ Remembering the instructions on page 18, you need to skim-read this section the first time in order to jot down an initial sentence, and then re-read it to refine this sentence and gather evidence to support it.

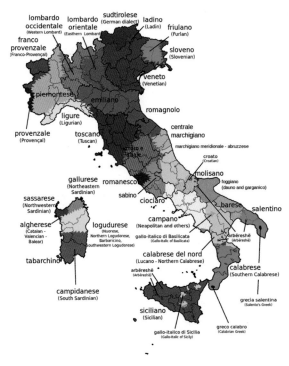

△ A map of Italian dialects and languages today, which shows the major groups of languages, including those of major regions such as Romanesco and Piedmontese. It also shows that many 'Italians' actually speak Greek, German, French or Slovenian. You do not need to know the names of all (or indeed any!) of these dialects – instead, you should be aware of the diversity of the spoken languages of Italy and understand the effects of this diversity.

Factor 4: Differences in language and culture

Only 2.5 per cent of the people living in Italy in 1815 actually spoke Italian. Even today, visitors to Italy find that Italians talk in very different ways in the various regions. What we know as 'Italian' is actually a Tuscan dialect, which emerged as a common language that Italians could use for literature and poetry in the fourteenth century. However, because it was developed for use in high literature, it was not the language of ordinary people. Through to the nineteenth century, ordinary 'Italians' continued to speak their own dialects, which might in some cases resemble Italian, but which often was much closer to ancient languages, such as Latin or Greek, or the language of groups such as the arbresche Albanians who, despite having settled in Italy since the fifteenth century still today maintain their own language. Even where the dialects had grown out of similar languages like Latin, Spanish or French, they were so different as to make communication between some areas very difficult.

These continuing language differences show how unchanging some groups were, and how little they travelled, or communicated with other areas of Italy. The fact that Italians did not speak with one language meant that they could not use language as a symbol of a common identity. Those that did speak and read Italian tended to be in the middle or upper classes, or come from Tuscany where 'Italian' originated. This meant that any notion of 'Italian-ness' that did arise from the language did not apply to the vast majority of Italians. When thinkers like Mazzini wrote about 'Italy' in order to persuade Italians that they should unite, not only did the thinkers write in a language that they had 'learned', but most of the people who they wanted to convince could not read the words they had written.

Factor 5: Class divisions

The Italian classes were not just divided by the lack of a common language.

The history of Italy and especially her recent history had led to power and land being concentrated in the hands of the aristocratic noble families. During the French occupation this process was accelerated as common land and land that had belonged to the Catholic Church was **enclosed** or sold to the nobles. This land was also increasingly sold to the new wealthy middle professional classes of lawyers, doctors and administrators. As Martin Clark puts it, 'in most cases the landlord's estates and their power over the peasants increased dramatically'.

Poverty was also increasing among many peasants. In Naples in the south and in some states in the north, peasants were unable to raise money to develop their land or found that their farms were not large or productive enough to work at a profit. These farmers were often forced to sell their land, which then ended up being bought by landowners and consolidated into larger farms. The peasants evicted from their land often became impoverished day labourers, known as *braccianti*. However, we have to be careful when making generalisations about Italy. In Piedmont, some peasants were able to rent or buy the land on which they worked. These peasants were often able to farm their land at a profit. These differences meant that peasants did not have a single agenda for change, or much interest in an idea like 'Italy' or 'unification'.

For the majority of peasants, life had in fact been getting worse for several generations, as the processes of change in land ownership carried on. The increasingly poor peasants, especially in the south, often rioted in protest at high grain prices or shortages of bread, and for some 'migration turned to brigandage' according to Stuart Woolf, as some who were starving turned to crime.

Throughout the period we are studying some enthusiasts for unification over-estimated how much support the idea of 'Italy' would get from Italian peasants. However, the increasing desperation of the peasants' conditions, coupled with the fear of the role that the peasantry had taken in the events of the French Revolution, led many in the middle and upper classes to fear peasants. Many saw them as a problem to be solved, rather than a group to enlist, persuade or work with. This suspicion was increased by some events during the French occupation, as in Naples in 1799, when French soldiers and administrators, along with Italians suspected of sympathising were massacred at the hands of a peasant mob led by Catholic Cardinal Ruffo. These fears made it very hard for those in the middle classes who wanted to bring change to Italy, to work with the 'backward' or 'primitive' peasants who made up the majority of the people in the peninsula.

◼ Have another look at the instructions on page 18 – remember to jot down your first thoughts after skimming through this section the first time, and to add your supporting evidence after re-reading it.

enclosed
Enclosure was the practice of fencing in common land. Previously common land had been available for the community to use as a source of grazing for cows, forage for pigs or firewood for people. This was seen as a wasteful use of land and in many countries enclosure gave ownership of such land to individuals in the hope that they would farm it more productively

△ Cardinal Ruffo's mobs murdered middle-class Italians who had worked with the French occupiers in 1799.

However, we have to guard against the idea that if the middle classes and peasants had joined forces then Italy would have been unified much earlier and in a much more effective way. Although there was a small but growing middle class in Italy, we cannot assume that the middle classes wanted to see a united Italy. Indeed, in some areas these middle-class professionals, lawyers, doctors and, more rarely, merchants and manufacturers, worked with their local aristocracy by taking positions as local administrators. In most cases these relationships were based on local power structures – positions in the state, or more usually in the city's administration, rather than in working together for a united Italy. While some middle-class idealists wrote for and read political journals, many also found advancement in local government. As the historian Lucy Riall puts it:

> … the powers allocated to local administration – the control over taxation, public works, bureaucratic appointments and, crucially, over the partition of common-land offered those in charge significant opportunities for patronage and for the accumulation of private wealth.

This process of the middle classes siding with the local noble elites was not a uniform one. In many smaller cities and towns such as Parma and Lucca, the aristocratic families managed to keep power without allying with the middle classes. However, in other states especially after the restoration in 1815, the local aristocracy itself was removed from local power as monarchs retained some of the centralised systems of taxation and administration that the French had introduced.

The most important point is that these alliances, struggles and conflicts were based around local, city and state administrative structures. This meant that in most cases arguments and disputes were about local issues and power struggles, not part of a movement designed to replace these structures with something that would lead to a united Italy.

■ Have you just read this section for the first time? Jot down your first ideas about how these differences contributed to Italian disunity. After the second reading you should record some key pieces of evidence to support this analysis.

Factor 6: The role of the Catholic Church

In some phases of Italian history, and for some enthusiasts of unification in the nineteenth century, it was hoped that the Catholic Church would provide a unifying force against foreign domination. The Catholic Church in Italy traces its history to the creation of the first Christian group by Saint Peter in Rome itself. During the Middle Ages the Church had asserted its temporal power over large parts of Europe, but since the Reformation and the **Enlightenment** her temporal power had shrunk to the Papal States.

However, the Church actively worked against the process of unification in the period we are studying in this book. Cardinals and priests had allied with peasants against French sympathisers and middle-class reformers during the Napoleonic occupation. The Church had lost power and land during that period, and had lost out in the restoration when not all her land and powers in the states had been restored. What authority remained to the Church outside the Papal States was bound up in local power structures. In Piedmont and in other states for instance, the Church ran the education system and still had her own set of **ecclesiastical courts**. All over the peninsula the Church was responsible for welfare and charity work. Unification would mean the end of the temporal power over the Papal States that remained to the Papacy, and most likely the introduction of liberal press and education laws that would see the Church lose much of her influence elsewhere in the peninsula.

Enlightenment
The Enlightenment was a period in which many scientists, philosophers and political thinkers developed new ideas which questioned traditional and accepted ways of thinking

ecclesiastical courts
Special law courts which heard cases involving priests or cases relating to religious crimes. They often gave lighter punishments to clergymen than other courts

■ This is the last section. Follow the instructions on page 18 to complete your note card.

■ Concluding your enquiry

You should now have six pieces of paper or index cards. Each one will contain a sentence of analysis or two explaining how the factor affected the unity of Italy. You will also have collected evidence to support your analysis of each factor. You will now use these cards to build an argument.

1 Re-read each card and then arrange them in a shape that best explains how these factors worked, together, to make unification unlikely before 1848.

 The shape that you arrange the cards in is up to you. Perhaps you think that this was a chain of factors, with one factor leading to another – in which case which card comes first? How does it link to the next?

2 Think about the relative importance of the factors in explaining why unification was unlikely. Some factors may be important because of the effect that they had on their own. Some factors might be important because they enabled or enhanced the effect of other factors. Perhaps one factor is the most significant because of its links to all the others – how could you show this by arranging the cards?

3 When you are happy with your chosen shape, stick the cards down on a piece of A3 paper and use the space around to explain your layout, and any links between the cards that you think help us to understand why unification was so unlikely.

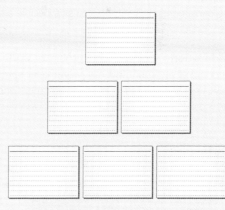

▷ Perhaps you think that the cards form a pyramid with the most important factor at the top, or even the most important 'foundation' factors at the bottom?

The failed revolutions of the 1820s and 1830s

Insight

Metternich may have hoped, and expected that Italy would remain quiet under Austrian domination. However, twice in the period before 1848 revolutions across the peninsula threatened Austrian's domination of Italy. In 1821, revolutionaries in Naples demanded, and achieved the granting of a constitution, while in Piedmont the King abdicated following a revolt by army officers.

Similarly, in 1831 revolts across Parma, Modena and the northern parts of the Papal States (known as the Romagna) also looked as if they might reach their goals. The cities of Bologna, Ancona and Perugia in the Romagna had thrown off the yoke of Papal rule and were starting to consider the creation of a **federation** of these cities. Revolutions also forced Duchess Marie Louise of Parma and Duke Francis IV of Modena from their thrones. At the very least it seemed that these states could expect **constitutional** rule and perhaps even a federation of Central Italy.

But the revolutions of 1820–21 and those of 1831 turned out to be failures. The only thing they seemed to show was how far off and difficult it would be to achieve independence from Austria, much less unification. Their failure exposed many weaknesses in the revolutionary movements, the extent of the rulers' fear that revolution would spread, and the lack of enthusiasm that most Italians felt towards the idea of 'Italy'.

Constitution – the rules that govern how a country is run. Many of these rules protect the rights of the citizens. The states of Italy had no constitutions in 1820. The rulers of each state theoretically had no limits on their powers within their boundaries and did not use things like parliaments or assemblies to give people a say in the running of their kingdoms and dukedoms.

Federation – federations are groups of states that agree to create a central government that has power over some things, but which leaves many important areas of government and decision making to the individual states. The United States of America is the most famous example.

Carbonari
The Carbonari was the most high profile of the secret societies which had started during the Napoleonic era as a way of resisting rule from France. They continued after 1815 as a way of resisting the Austrian domination of Italy. These societies attracted thousands of members, especially from the middle and minor-aristocratic classes. Their aims were vague, many calling for constitutions to be granted in their states, but some members were more radical, and hoped for Italian unification

Revolutions of 1820–21

Naples, 1820

This rebellion against King Ferdinand of Naples was led by the **Carbonari** and members of the army, and demanded a constitution. It was inspired by the successes of a revolt in Spain which had seen the introduction of a constitution there. Eventually King Ferdinand was forced to grant such a constitution. However, after tricking his new government to let him travel to Austria, Ferdinand asked for Austrian military help in ending the revolt.

Sicily, 1820

Shortly after the start of the revolts in Naples trouble spread to Sicily where separatist rebels demanded independence from Naples. Most of the action was limited to the capital, Palermo. The newly formed Neapolitan government, scared that the unrest would cause Austria to intervene, and worried that Sicily might gain its independence from Naples, sent military force to Sicily to crush the revolution.

Piedmont, 1821

In Piedmont, army officers, under the leadership of a young aristocrat, Santorre di Santarosa seized the fortress of Alessandria and declared a provisional government, calling for the King's cousin, Charles Albert to replace the ageing King Victor Emmanuel. Victor Emmanuel abdicated in favour of his brother, Charles Felix, who was abroad. Charles Albert therefore briefly ruled until the return of the new king. When Charles Felix returned he immediately asked Austria for military support in ending the revolts, which were then crushed by Austrian and Piedmontese troops.

Revolutions of 1831

Papal States, 1831

In February 1831 revolutions started in the city of Bologna, because of resentment at rule from Rome, which meant that senior priests held power in the city and the region. The revolts spread quickly to other cities in this northern part of the Papal States, including Ancona and Perugia. All the revolts were quickly mopped up by Austrian and Papal troops.

Modena and Parma, 1831

Conspirators planned to make Francesco IV of Modena King of Italy, and thought that they had secured his agreement. However, in early March Francesco then betrayed the plot to the Austrians and had the leaders of the conspiracy arrested. Francesco fled to Vienna and appealed to Metternich, the Chancellor of Austria, for help in ending the revolts in his state. Duchess Marie Louise of Parma fled also, fearing the spread of revolutions to her state. By March the revolts had been brought to an end by Austrian troops.

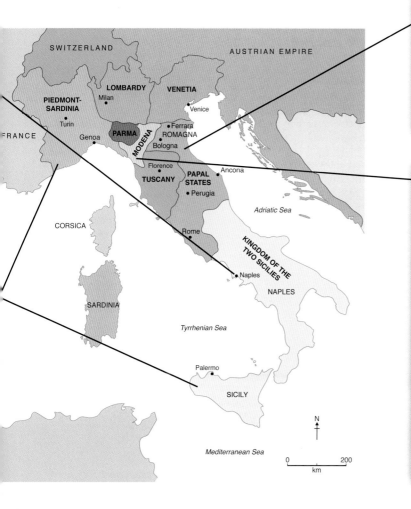

SWITZERLAND

AUSTRIAN EMPIRE

LOMBARDY
Milan

VENETIA

PIEDMONT-
SARDINIA

Venice

Turin

FRANCE

PARMA

MODENA

Ferrara
ROMAGNA

Genoa

Bologna

Florence

Ancona

TUSCANY

PAPAL
STATES

Perugia

Adriatic Sea

CORSICA

Rome

KINGDOM OF THE
TWO SICILIES

Naples

NAPLES

SARDINIA

Tyrrhenian Sea

Palermo

SICILY

N

Mediterranean Sea

0   200
km

Why did the revolutions of 1820–21 and 1831 fail so completely?

Were the revolutions of 1820–21 and 1831 stepping stones to unification?

Hopefully, by reading about the factors which caused the failure of these revolts you have understood the reasons and circumstances which saw Charles Felix of Piedmont, Ferdinand I of Naples and the Pope restored to their positions as **absolute monarchs** after these revolts. Could any of these factors have been changed or overcome during these revolts? We think that this was unlikely – though we do not see the outcome as inevitable.

absolute monarch
An absolute monarch is one who rules without a constitution and with no restrictions on their ability to make laws or exercise their power. They do not have parliaments and their citizens cannot take part in government.

Lack of unified aims for the revolts

These revolutions grew out of simmering discontent among some of the middle classes, who were finding it difficult to get jobs in government, the law and other professions. Educated graduates of Italian universities, young men qualified in law and medicine, working in the armies of the Italian states or in their governments during the Napoleonic period found that they had been pushed aside in the restoration of the monarchy. They had gained wealth and status under Napoleon and were not happy that so much of their power was lost at the restoration in 1815.

However, the revolutionaries did not have a common set of ideas about how things should change. Some held quite radical views, thinking that Italy ought to be a united country with a democratic system of government in which ordinary people could vote. Most would have preferred their own kings and dukes to remain in power, but as constitutional rather than absolute monarchs without the influence of Austria, and with lots more opportunities for middle-class jobs within each state government. Many were suspicious of 'foreigners', the name they gave to those from other Italian states, or even from their neighbouring cities. We can see this in the 1831 revolts where leaders of the revolts in Bologna refused a request to join forces from those in nearby Modena. Similarly, in the 1821 revolts the leaders of the revolution in the Kingdom of Naples were divided. On the island of Sicily the leaders wanted Sicilian independence – they didn't want to be ruled by Naples at all.

Lack of support from ordinary 'Italians'

Even Mazzini, an Italian revolutionary who had great hopes that the people of Italy would rise up and free themselves, had to admit that they 'remained inert, indifferent and without faith in the future' during the revolts of 1831, and this was also the case in the revolts of 1820–21. The hopes for independence for Sicily shows us that some Italians did not want unification, but most ordinary Italians would not have even considered that unification might be possible, much less given it their support. As we have seen in the last chapter, most ordinary peasants would have been more concerned with growing enough food or earning enough money to keep their families fed. It was no coincidence that 1848, the year in which many peasants did take part in revolts, came after two years of bad harvests and an economic depression.

Lack of support from foreign powers

In 1821, soon after the revolts in Naples and Sicily, Austria called a 'congress' (a meeting) between the French, British, Austrians, Prussians and Russians in Troppau, a city in the Austrian Empire. At that meeting the Troppau protocol was signed. This agreement held that the Great Powers should intervene, to stop rebellions from being successful. The agreement was signed by Austria, Prussia and Russia, the three countries who had the most power on the continent. Britain and France did not sign, but France was still unable (after her defeat in 1815) to try to push for more influence. Britain might have welcomed constitutional rule in Naples, but her statesmen decided that the British interest was best served by maintaining the 'balance of power' – in that a strong Austria contained the ambitions of Russia and France. Therefore they did not attempt to stop the Austrians when they put down the revolts in Naples.

On the other hand, we have also seen that sometimes, when looking at history, we can make the mistake of seeing an overall story where there isn't one. Sometimes these early revolts are seen as stepping stones to unification – we hope that you can see that this was not really the case. These revolts confirmed the settlement of 1815, and in particular confirmed Austria's dominant role over the peninsula. Very little could change while Austria held on to this power.

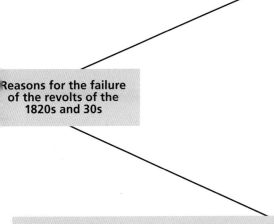

Poor leadership

The leaders of the revolts made many mistakes. For instance, in Naples they relented when Ferdinand asked to go to meet the Austrians, following the Troppau protocol. Ferdinand promised that he would defend the new constitution. As soon as he was safely away from Naples, Ferdinand asked the Austrian Emperor for help in quashing the rebellion and restoring autocratic rule in Naples and Sicily. At the same time, when the rebels in Naples and Sicily might have been working together, preparing for the invasion that might (and indeed did) come from Austria, Naples and Sicily fought each other. Metternich quickly sent the troops that Ferdinand requested and by March they succeeded in restoring Ferdinand's absolute powers. However, this was not the end of revolution in 1821. Santarosa was naïve in thinking that the people of Piedmont would back a revolution against the Austrians and put Charles Albert in a very difficult position. Similarly in the 1831 revolts, the leaders were foolish in thinking that they could use the Duke of Modena against the Austrians, when his position as duke depended on Austrian support.

Reasons for the failure of the revolts of the 1820s and 30s

Austrian power

We should also bear in mind that it was the Austrians who provided the military power that ended the revolts of 1820–21 and 1831. They were able to do this with the approval of the Prussians and Russians, the tacit permission of the British and the French and the invitation of the legitimate rulers of the states of Naples and Piedmont. The Austrians' position of power was therefore not just based on their military might but also on the legitimacy of their actions. This military power, and the way that it was made more legitimate by the Vienna Settlement and the Troppau protocol, was the most serious barrier to change in Italy in the years before 1848. Indeed, as we shall see, even in that revolutionary year, when Austrian power itself seemed to falter, even then she was strong enough to crush the revolts across Italy.

3 Which ideas about Italy's future were most likely to win support by 1848?

△ Born in 1805, Mazzini was an influential thinker and radical Italian politician.

Though the revolts in 1820–21 and 1831 had been easily crushed, they did leave a lasting legacy in the minds of a generation of thinkers, such as Giuseppe Mazzini, who came after them. Much later Mazzini explained in his memoirs how an event in 1821 inspired his nationalism. As you read the extract below try to identify what it was about this event that had such an influence on the 16-year-old Mazzini.

One Sunday in April 1821, while I was yet a boy, I was walking in the Strada Nuova of Genoa, with my mother. The [1821 revolts in Piedmont] had just been crushed, partly by Austria, partly through treachery and partly through the weakness of its leaders. The revolutionaries, seeking [to escape] by sea, had flocked to Genoa […] and went about looking for help to enable them to cross into Spain, where another revolt still went on.

We were stopped by a tall black-bearded man with a severe and energetic face and a fiery glance that I have never since forgotten. He held out a white handkerchief towards us, merely saying 'for the refugees of Italy'. My mother dropped some money into his handkerchief.

That day an idea presented itself to my mind, not yet of country or of liberty, but an idea that we Italians could and therefore should struggle for the liberty of our country.

This extract not only shows Mazzini's great skill as a writer and the nature of some of his ideas, but also identifies three important influences on his life. The first of these was his childhood home in Genoa. This is interesting, because before the invasions and occupations during the wars with Napoleonic France (1792–1815), Genoa had been an independent city-state, a Republic in which the wealthy in the city voted for its leaders. However, after the destruction caused by these French Revolutionary Wars, republican ideas were out of favour with the Great Powers and in 1815, instead of being restored to independence (as were some of the other states of Italy), Genoa was instead made part of Piedmont. This caused a great deal of resentment in the city, especially among the middle classes who lost power and influence under the Piedmontese monarchy. Genoa, therefore, became a hot-bed of radicals and Carbonari. Mazzini was part of this tradition.

Mazzini also mentioned the influence of his mother. He was never to see her again after 1831 when he was exiled from Italy after a prison sentence for revolutionary activity. However, he was very close to her, and until she died in 1852 she sent gifts of clothes and money (most of which he gave away to revolutionary friends) to Paris or to London, where he spent his exile. Some of this generosity in Mazzini and his mother can also be seen in the extract on page 34. The third influence you might have noted was Mazzini's love of ideas – especially those of 'liberty' and 'nation', which came forcibly to his mind as he stared at the imposing 'black-bearded' revolutionary hero, and which were already informing his belief in unification.

The Enlightenment, Romanticism and Italy

Mazzini was fascinated by the romantic idea of 'nation', and saw the potential in romantic art forms to inspire the people of Italy to rise up against the Austrians. His hopes of a united Italy should also be seen in the context of the Enlightenment, which inspired ideas of progress and reform that would lead to greater happiness and prosperity. The Enlightenment and Romanticism were two sets of ideas that developed across Europe in the eighteenth and nineteenth centuries, each of which had an important effect on the way that people thought about other important ideas such as 'nation' and 'people'.

The Enlightenment

The Enlightenment grew out of an earlier revolution in scientific thought in the seventeenth century, in which philosophers and scientists abandoned the idea that religion or tradition could explain how the world worked. The leading Enlightenment philosopher, David Hume, wrote in 1689 that 'A wise man ... proportions his belief to the evidence'. This quotation illustrates the importance that Enlightenment thinkers placed upon having evidence to make a statement. Many such thinkers sought to explain the world by gathering evidence about it, by observing and experimenting. The Enlightenment made some Italian thinkers more likely to question why things were the way they were, and to suggest changes, rather than just accept the status quo. The Enlightenment also had a 'universalising' effect on the way intellectuals thought – it tended to stress the similarities between different groups of people. This had the potential to show Italians that they had much in common. The scientific emphasis of the Enlightenment led people to want to re-organise society, usually along what they thought as being scientific and rational grounds. The ideas of the Enlightenment therefore inspired some Italians to press for change.

Romanticism

Romanticism, which flourished in the late eighteenth century, was partly a reaction against the 'rational' Enlightenment. Romantics emphasised sense, feelings and intuition, as opposed to science and rational thought, and the Romantic approach is reflected in these lines from William Wordsworth's poem 'The Prelude', published in 1799:

> Fair seed-time had my soul, and I grew up
>
> Fostered alike by beauty and by fear:
>
> Much favoured in my birthplace …

△ *The Wanderer above the Sea of Fog* by German artist, Caspar David Friedrich. This picture sums up some of the main themes of Romanticism – individual genius, the force of nature, and lonely contemplation.

Romanticism developed the idea of national character, of the differences between countries. In particular, some romantic thinkers focused on the idea that language and geography moulded certain traits and gave different strengths, weaknesses and even destinies to different national groups. This was especially true for Italy, where in comparison to other countries Romantic artists had an even greater focus on the formation of national characteristics and on Italy's classical, Roman history. Opera, like that composed by Verdi, became particularly popular with the upper and middle classes in Italy. Its themes of nation, threats from barbarians and invasion, of sacrifice and heroism, could also be seen in literature and helped create a sense of nationalism in some Italians. Many were inspired by such ideas to make daring attempts at revolts, and Romanticism encouraged many young Italian men to risk their lives in the cause of Italian independence and unification. However, we should remind ourselves that these young men were a very small minority of the Italian people, most of whom were unmoved by ideas of nation or of sacrificing themselves for Italy.

The lack of development of political culture in Italy

Mazzini, like others influenced by the Enlightenment and Romanticism, wanted to create a new Italian nation. However, he faced a very difficult task – not least because there was no clear tradition of political union in Italy in the early nineteenth century. Since the end of the Roman Empire in the late fifth century AD, Italy had been divided. Even in the Middle Ages, a time of great influence and success, it was Italian cities that were successful, not Italy as a whole. Italian cities therefore had a fierce tradition of independence. Their governments had been dominated by fabulously wealthy local merchants who resented interference from outside, and who battled with the merchant-aristocracies of other cities over trade routes and territory.

In the Renaissance period in the fifteenth and sixteenth centuries Italy's political independence vanished. In a series of wars Spanish and French forces fought over the peninsula until Spanish victory was confirmed. From the mid-sixteenth century, Spain dominated the peninsula, using traditional **feudal aristocracies** to maintain power on behalf of Spanish dukes and kings. This change had several effects on the political structure of Italy, the main ones being that local noble landowners had increased power, and that loyalties of peasants often lay with leading local families, rather than with even the Dukedom or Kingdom in which they lived, let alone with any idea of 'Italy' as a whole.

Economic recession and stagnating trade from the eighteenth century onwards meant that the middle classes did not develop in the same way that they did in countries like England and Germany. As a result, the middle classes, who might be expected to have been more attracted by the idea of a united Italy, had much less political influence than they did in other places in Europe. Italy therefore, remained divided.

While by the early nineteenth century Italy was more stable, this tradition of independence and local control remained so that after 1815 it was still a divided peninsula but of states rather than cities. These states continued to have different laws and different political traditions, all of which helps to explain how difficult the task of creating a new united Italian nation would be.

feudal aristocracy
Rule by an 'aristocratic' or noble class over small states, dukedoms and kingdoms, with only weak influence from a central authority

---

■ **Enquiry Focus:** Which ideas about Italy's future were most likely to win support by 1848?

This enquiry focuses on the ideas about Italy's future that emerged following the unsuccessful revolts of 1831. These ideas can be categorised as either about:

a) **Unification** – a single unified state with the same laws across the whole peninsula, and for many thinkers, with a republican, democratic constitution.

b) **Confederation** – a unified 'country', but one in which the states retain a good deal of power and independence, with a much weaker central government. There were different opinions about who should lead any 'Italian Confederation'.

Your task in part 1 of this enquiry is to read about the ideas of three men – Mazzini, Balbo and Gioberti – and summarise their ideas in the table below. In addition, make detailed notes to support the summary in the table. Don't worry if you are not sure about which groups might support each man's ideas as we shall return to this issue in part 2 of the enquiry.

	Did he support unification or confederation?	If confederation, who did he believe should lead the confederation?	Which social groups were most likely to support his ideas?
Mazzini			
Balbo			
Gioberti			

In part 2 of this enquiry you will look in more detail at the attitudes of four social groups – the peasantry, the Church, the middle classes and the aristocracy – and decide then which of these ideas was most likely to win the most influential support.

△ Mazzini spent most of his life in exile after 1931 following a prison sentence for revolutionary activity. He died in 1872.

Part 1: The ideas

1. Mazzini's 'Young Italy'

Mazzini, whom we met at the start of this chapter, believed in Italy, as a nation. Where others saw Neapolitans, Sicilians, Bolognese, Piedmontese and Romans, Mazzini saw Italians. In his 'Manifesto of Young Italy', published in 1831, he wrote that 'the whole problem consists in appealing to the true instincts and tendencies of the Italian heart'. Mazzini believed that Italy was one nation, with an Italian spirit, and that this nation would one day rise up and, in the heat of a revolution, throw off Austrian domination and forge a new, unified Italian state.

Mazzini's vision was inspired by the mood of Romanticism and grew out of his conviction that Italy had a glorious Roman and Renaissance past which should be used to inspire a new unified future. Indeed, Mazzini saw a role for this new Italy in leading a Europe of Nations, in which each national group had a special role to play.

In October 1831, frustrated by the failure of the revolutions in Romagna and in Modena that year, and inspired by the sacrifice made by those who took part in these revolts, Mazzini formed Young Italy, a secret society dedicated to revolution. He described this society as aiming for a 'republic and unity, because the Italian tradition is entirely republican. Unity because without unity there is no strength'.

As we can see, Young Italy was dedicated to the founding of a republican, democratic, unified Italian state. For us democracy means 'one vote for every adult', but Mazzini was quite vague about what it meant for him, suggesting that only those educated enough to understand their duty should be able to vote. We would see this as a very restrictive view of the electorate, but in nineteenth century Italy this seemed like a very radical idea.

From the start Mazzini wanted Young Italy to be a 'mass' political movement – he wanted ordinary Italians to take part, and he saw that this would mean changing the attitudes of most people, alongside organising revolution. This is clear from the manifesto, which tells us that 'The means by which Young Italy proposes to reach its aim are education and **insurrection**'. Mazzini was convinced that it was the apathy of the mass of Italian people that had led to the failures of the 1820 and 1831 revolutions, and indeed that this apathy had given Italy over to foreign domination. He wanted peasants to be persuaded of their Italian nationality and to play a part in a national revolution, which would get rid of the Austrians, and the rulers of the different states in Italy. He believed that only by working together as Italians could they hope to destroy Austria's power and make this new country.

Making the peasantry more politically active was a difficult task though. Their lack of education, indeed the control of education in most states by the Church, meant that peasants were mostly illiterate, and so immune to the passionate writing that Mazzini produced in the Young Italy Journal. This was published infrequently (just six times between 1832 and 1834) from across the border in Marseilles, France.

insurrection
A revolt or uprising against a government – it is usually violent and sudden

Mazzini's ideas did inspire more foolhardy Italian patriots to launch brave and risky attempts at revolutions. The Bandiera brothers' attempt to start a revolution in Calabria in 1844 is a good example. These two minor aristocrats from Venice gathered a group of revolutionaries on the island of Corfu. In spring 1844 they set off with just over 20 men, hoping that when they landed in Calabria in the far south of the Italian peninsula, the locals would rise up alongside them and start a revolution. Instead, they were attacked by a local mob, several were shot and the survivors (including the Bandieras) were arrested, put on trial by King Ferdinand and executed by firing squad.

Mazzini's reputation might have remained as that of a revolutionary hothead, an inspirer of brave and foolish expeditions, had it not been for the part he later played in the 1848 revolutions and the defence of the Roman Republic, which we will look at in the next chapter.

■ Fill in the table to record your thinking. Would Mazzini have supported the idea of a confederation or of unity? Would Mazzini's ideas have appealed to others? Think about:

- What are the main elements in Mazzini's plan for a revived Italy?
- Which groups might feel threatened by his ideas?
- Which groups might welcome them?

---

2. Cesare Balbo's 'Hope of Italy'

In 1844, Cesare Balbo wrote:

> Confederations are the type of constitutions most suited to Italy's nature and history. The serious obstacle to an Italian confederation is foreign rule, which penetrates deep inside the peninsula. [...] The princes can do nothing without the peoples, they are not really princes unless they can persuade their people to act. However, this doesn't mean that democratic revolution is likely to succeed in Italy, though many in the secret societies want it, and those in the police fear it. The Kings of Piedmont have upheld a sacred fire of Italian virtue for half a century, and in that time have doubled their territory and population, all at the expense of Austria.

△ Cesare Balbo (1789–1853) was a member of a minor aristocratic family who had served in Napoleon's Empire. He became a writer to encourage Italy to free itself from Austrian influence.

Cesare Balbo was part of a group of Piedmontese political moderates (including Massimo d'Azeglio, later to be Prime Minister of Piedmont) who came from aristocratic families. As you can see from the extract above, some moderates like Balbo pinned their hopes for change in Italy on the House of Savoy, the ruling family of Piedmont. For Balbo and his followers, the House of Savoy's 'sacred fire of Italian virtue' showed that Italians could fight, could be loyal, and could run an effective and efficient state.

Balbo's ideas were much less radical than Mazzini's. He was very sceptical of the idea of inspiring the mass of Italian peasants, whom he regarded as lazy and effeminate. He believed that Italy could not be forced to become one unified country because the differences between the states

See page 58 for more details about moderates' and radicals' ideas for Italy.

The United States
of America became
a 'federal' republic
in 1789. Under this
federation, power
was shared between
the individual states
of the Union, and
a central 'federal'
government.

It was Balbo who
first suggested that
Austria might obtain
territory further east,
in the Balkans, in
order to compensate
for the loss of land in
Lombardy–Venetia.
See page 101.

were too great. His goal, therefore, was a federation of independent states with only a measure of central power held by a national government, rather than full unity with a national government that decided policy for the whole country.

Under Balbo's plan, each state would retain its rulers (who would keep most of their powers) and its own laws and customs, but would look to other states to lead in certain areas like trade, the military or culture. Italy's states could therefore remain proud of their differences. **Federation** seemed like a powerful new idea because it had been used successfully in the USA after the War of Independence from Britain (1775–83). At the head of this federation would be the Piedmontese King, who would lead 'Italy', especially in teaching them how to fight, so that independence from foreigners could be assured. Balbo saw Piedmont as the military example for the rest of the Italians because Piedmont had a fairly modern army (with about 150,000 soldiers), and a strong monarchy.

Balbo believed that military leadership was needed because it was foreign domination, and Austrian domination in particular, that was holding back change in the Italian peninsula. But he also saw that Austria would have to be persuaded to leave its possessions in Italy and that international allies would be needed to help in this persuasion. Although Balbo's ideas were popular with many members of the middle classes throughout Italy, not everyone was convinced that Piedmont's king was the ideal person to lead a united Italy. During the 1840s, Piedmontese moderates had persuaded King Charles Albert of Piedmont that their ideas might work and increasingly the Piedmontese King made hesitant reforms that seemed to suggest he was a liberal-leaning monarch. In reality his policy was designed to help minimise the risk of revolution, and to expand his influence, and the territory of Piedmont. Charles Albert hoped that the loyalty of the moderates might help him do this. Though Charles Albert met d'Azeglio in 1844 and claimed that his 'life, the life of my children, my arms, my treasure, my army, all will be spent for the Italian cause', d'Azeglio remained very sceptical of Charles's commitment to the cause of Italy.

Fill in the table to record your thoughts about Balbo's ideas and who they might appeal to. Think about:

- What are the main elements in his plan for a revived Italy?
- Which groups might feel threatened by his ideas?
- Which groups might welcome them?

3. Gioberti's 'The Moral Primacy of the Italians'

Italy has within herself all the conditions of her national and political *Risorgimento* without the need for revolution or foreign domination. The main force of Italian Unity is the Pope, who can unify the peninsula by means of a confederation. Two provinces should co-operate in Italy's unity – Rome and Piedmont.

△ Vincenzo Gioberti (1801–52) was a Catholic priest who had been exiled in 1834 because of his radical views. He taught and wrote in universities in Paris and Brussels before returning to Italy in 1847.

In 1843, Gioberti's book *The Moral and Civil Primacy of the Italians* set out his hopes of a re-born Italy, free from the control of foreigners. Gioberti saw himself as a pragmatic political thinker – there was no point, for him and his followers, in dreaming up what a perfect Italy might look like in the future; they had to take into account what Italy was really like. This meant they realised that her recent history and culture would affect the future that they were planning.

Like Mazzini, Gioberti was heavily influenced by Romantic ideas – and he too saw a special past and a special role for the 'Italian' nation, in which Italy would lead the world in civilisation and morals (which is what Gioberti meant by 'moral primacy'). Gioberti also saw history as a way of inflaming national passion in the hearts of Italians. Unlike Mazzini, his history of Italy focused on the role of the Papacy in giving spiritual and intellectual leadership to the world and this greatly influenced his view of Italy's future.

Like his friend Cesare Balbo, Gioberti saw a federation as the way forward. But unlike Balbo, he hoped the Pope would lead this federation, and lead the states of Italy out of foreign domination. Gioberti agreed that the Italians had many differences, but he also saw that they had a very important thing in common – the Catholic faith. He argued that the Pope and the Papacy was the only force capable of bringing Italians together and inspiring them to throw off foreign domination. This idea was called '**neo-Guelphism**', because it was very similar to a medieval political movement among Italian noblemen known as 'Guelphs'. Medieval Guelphs were determined to support the Pope and to resist domination by the German Empire.

Neo-Guelphists
People who hoped that the Pope would rule a united, federal Italy

In some ways this was convincing – the Catholic Church was one of the few things that people had in common across the peninsula, and the Pope's religious leadership meant that he had the respect of many Italians. Gioberti's idea was also popular with these moderates who wanted to maintain the power that individual rulers held over their states – most powers would remain in the hands of these rulers under Gioberti's plan.

There were two problems with this idea though. The first was that the Church was not popular with many liberals. The Popes ruled as 'absolute' monarchs – you'll remember that it was this that led some members of the middle classes in Bologna to rebel against the Pope in 1831. This meant that many of the people who were pressing for change were unlikely to accept the leadership of the Pope.

The second problem was that although Gioberti saw a great future where the Pope was the head of a united Italy, he had no idea of how to get to that future. Gioberti didn't say how Italians were to persuade the

Peasant farmers made up the vast majority of the Italian population. They farmed to live, and paid a landowner for the use of the land on which they farmed.

Traditionally they had relied on communal land to graze animals or as a place to gather wood as fuel for heating. This was a hard life, made harder by disease, bad harvests and by the process of enclosure which saw private landowners take over communal land. Increasingly, in the south many peasants were unable to make money out of farming their own land because of falling prices, poor farming practice and the enclosure of common land. They became *braccianti* – day labourers who worked, when they could, for low wages.

For all their poverty, the huge numbers of the peasantry made them a very important group, especially to the more radical thinkers who wanted Italy to be free of Austrian domination and to become a unified republic. As we have already seen, Mazzini saw the 'education' of the peasants as very important in convincing them of their 'Italian' heritage and character. If the peasants were to rise up, they would then, reformers hoped, demand unification. This, of course, made other more moderate, liberal reformers afraid of making peasants more politically active – especially when they remembered that peasant risings in the early years of the French Occupation in Piedmont copied the language of the **French Revolution**. More conservative reformers who supported the ideas of Balbo or of Gioberti would have hoped that any form of Italian unity would be one in which peasants were persuaded to work and live peacefully without becoming politically active.

For information on the impact of the **French Revolution**, see pages 14–15.

However, when peasants did take political action this gave little hope to those seeking the creation of a united Italian nation. For instance, a peasant army, headed by a Catholic Cardinal, Ruffo, had helped push back French forces from Naples 1799. In the process they committed terribly brutal acts of murder and torture against the middle class and aristocratic Neapolitans who had worked with the French. It is important to note that the language Ruffo used to inspire the peasants had little to do with Italy. Referring to brave 'Calabrians' (the area of Italy in which the revolt started) rather than Italians, Ruffo called on the peasants to support the Pope and the King of Naples. He also used the resentment that many peasants felt against the middle classes that had supported the French. The peasants themselves shouted 'Long live the King', referring to the King of Naples. This is an example of the parochialism of peasant politics, but also of the power of the Church and religious symbols to move the peasants to action. All this suggested that, for the peasantry, the power of their local church and of their landlord, was far more important than ideas of Italian unity. This is one of the reasons why Gioberti believed that only the Catholic Church could inspire enough loyalty from most ordinary Italians to be able to act as a symbol of a confederated Italy.

> **1** Make detailed notes on the attitudes of the peasantry towards the idea of the unification or confederation of Italy. Why might some support the idea of unity? Why might others fear or dislike the idea of a united Italy? Would the peasants have seen much future for a confederation in Italy?
>
> **2** Add brief notes to your table to summarise these points, using the instructions on page 43.

The attitude of the Catholic Church to Italy's future

The Catholic Church suffered greatly during the Napoleonic occupation of Italy, the last time the peninsula had seen some unification. Church land was confiscated and sold. Also, Napoleon claimed the power to appoint bishops and to control education and welfare in the Empire, two things that the Church had traditionally overseen. In 1808–09 the French invaded the Papal States, arrested the Pope and ended his temporal power. As we saw above, religious symbols and Catholic clerics could be a powerful force in motivating peasants to take action against these changes.

After the restoration in 1815 the Papacy therefore had two important aims:

- To affirm the status of the Pope as ruler in the Papal States and to resist any change that might weaken either his rule, or the Papal States themselves.
- To re-assert its independence from the European powers, even from Austria.

Pope Pius VII issued a set of laws called a ***motu proprio*** in which he set out how the Papal States were to be ruled. They confirmed the absolute power of the Pope, and in fact removed the last feudal powers and taxes that the nobility had benefited from. Cardinals and priests regained their position as governors, judges and administrators across the Papal States. As we can see, these changes confirmed the Pope's role as the absolute ruler of the Papal States, and left little room for the possibility of unification; especially democratic unification as desired by Mazzini.

As we have seen in Chapter 2, rulers elsewhere in Italy relied on the Catholic Church as part of the machinery of government – often they were in charge of schools in each state. To that extent the Church was in a position to offer leadership in the way that Gioberti set out in his thinking. However, the Papacy needed to rely on Austria to provide military support against revolution. As we have seen, Austrian military power was indeed used in 1831 to restore the Pope's rule in the **Papal Legations**. The Papacy was therefore unable and unwilling to do anything to threaten Austria's power. As a result, the Papacy was resented by many radical reformers, like Mazzini, who saw it as part of the machinery of repression that prevented change in Italy. Even many moderate liberals like Balbo would have been wary of the effect of the Catholic Church on the attitudes of Italians towards change and 'progress' in Italy.

These developments tell us that the Pope and the Cardinals, who advised him and helped him to run the Papal States, were determined to maintain the status of the Papal States as a separate kingdom, with the Pope as an autocratic ruler. What is more, we can see that the security of the Papal States relied on the domination of Austria and the continuation of the 1815 Vienna Settlement.

motu proprio
A legal document in the form of a letter used by the Papacy to clarify rules or to set out how laws should work

Papal Legations
These were the cities and surrounding territories in the northern part of the Papal States such as Ferrara and Bologna

---

1 Make detailed notes on the attitudes of the Catholic Church towards the idea of Italy. Why might some support the idea of unity? Why might others in the Church fear or dislike the idea of a united Italy? Could the Church support the idea of 'confederation'?

2 Add brief notes to your table to summarise these points, using the instructions on page 43.

The attitude of the middle classes to Italy's future

We have already seen that some members of the middle class had done well out of the Napoleonic occupation of Italy either as administrators, as officers in the army of Italy or as a result of buying up Church land sold cheaply to them by the French regime. However, at the Restoration in 1815, many of these individuals had been pushed out of important government jobs and positions of influence. In resentment some joined secret sects like the **Carbonari**, and worked to bring change to Italian states in the revolts of the 1820s and 1830s. Others were influenced by Romantic novels, paintings, opera and poetry which made it fashionable to flirt with ideas of nation.

See page 30 for information on the **Carbonari**.

However, we should be careful not to lump all the middle classes together. The split between moderate and more radical, democratic rebels in the 1821 revolts in Naples tells us that many in the middle classes were suspicious of democracy. In addition, few of the radicals or moderates who took part in the revolts of 1821 and 1831 demanded the unification of Italy, nor even the independence of Italy as a whole from Austrian domination. They simply wanted to have more influence in their own states. As we learned from looking at the Carbonari (page 30), most middle-class Italians were more interested in reforms that would increase their say and influence in their own states and give them opportunities to make money through trade and industry. Even the small minority of the middle-classes who were enthusiastic about the idea of a united Italy looked at this from the point of view of their own state taking a leading role. It seems that middle-class 'Italians' who wanted 'progress' saw their own state as a way of increasing their own influence – they would not have wanted their states to disappear in a unified, centralised Italian state. This would suggest that they would prefer to support ideas of confederation, like those of Gioberti or of Balbo.

However, we should also remember that liberal ideas often went hand-in-hand with suspicion of the Church's role in government and **anti-clericalism** though many were committed religious believers. The middle classes who agreed with many liberal ideas saw religion as a private affair that the state should not interfere with – and that a religious leader should not hold political power.

anti-clericalism
A suspicion of the role of priests and other clergy, especially when they have political power

---

1. Make detailed notes on the attitudes of the middle classes towards the idea of the unification or confederation of Italy. Why might some support the idea of unity? Why might others fear or dislike the idea? Would a confederation appeal to some members of the middle classes?

2. Add brief notes to your table to summarise these points, using the instructions on page 43.

The attitudes of local rulers and aristocracies to Italy's future

Monarchy – centralised power in the hands of one person – was the idea that dominated the restoration and Vienna Settlement of 1815. While this idea strengthened the position of the rulers – the dukes and monarchs of the states of the Italian peninsula, it also meant the weakening of the powers, rights and traditions of the nobles in many of these states, especially those of the north – Lombardy, Venetia, Piedmont and the Papal States.

In Lombardy some nobles with intellectual interests turned to literature and history to try to revive the national spirit of Italy. They published a journal, called *The Conciliator* which included articles about history, politics and literature and offered visions of a rejuvenated Italy (though it is likely that by 'Italy', its authors meant the northern Kingdom of Italy that had briefly existed during the Napoleonic period), which implied independence from Austria. Unsurprisingly this journal was increasingly censored by the Austrian authorities.

In Piedmont, nobles showed loyalty to the House of Savoy (the family of the Kings of Piedmont-Sardinia) because of its status as an Italian dynasty independent from Austria. The House of Savoy also had a **military tradition**. Even rebels, such as Santarosa in 1820, as we have seen, looked to the King of Piedmont for military leadership to help expel Austria from northern Italy. Indeed, the Great Powers of 1815 had also put their faith in the Kingdom of Piedmont-Sardinia, which had been enlarged and strengthened by the Congress of Vienna, in the hope that it would be strong enough to form a 'buffer state' against the threat of French aggression.

However, the kings of Piedmont-Sardinia had showed themselves to be very conservative – after 1815 Victor Emmanuel I sought even to destroy the French roads and laws that Napoleon had brought during the French occupation. His successors were just as conservative, even Charles Albert who seemed to support the revolutions of 1821, repressed Mazzinian revolts in Piedmont when he came to power in 1831 and supported Austria's military crushing of a revolution in Switzerland. Although there was no guarantee that support for change in Italy would come from the House of Savoy, as we have seen from the actions of Charles Albert in 1821, there was evidence that the Kings of Piedmont might take opportunities to expand Piedmont's influence, power and perhaps her territory.

> Monarchies with a military tradition often maintain a standing army with which they have strong links, holding important positions in the army's hierarchy, taking key decisions about the development of their forces and an active role in fighting alongside their troops.

1 Make detailed notes on the attitudes of the aristocratic and ruling classes, towards the idea of Italy. Why might some support the idea of unity? Why might others fear or dislike the idea?

2 Add brief notes to your table to summarise these points, using the instructions on page 43.

You should now be able to suggest reasons why some of the groups we have covered might be drawn to some of the ideas for a 'new' Italy, while at the same time be fearful of the others. You should also have realised that some people in Italy would have resisted change to the 1815 settlement.

3 Re-read your earlier notes from part 1 and part 2. For each of the groups below write a brief explanation of the attitudes they might have to the ideas of Mazzini, Balbo and Gioberti. For instance, you could easily find that some people in each group might welcome one of the ideas, while others might welcome another of them.

- Peasants
- The Catholic Church
- The middle classes
- Local rulers and aristocrats

Concluding your enquiry: Which ideas about Italy's future were most likely to win support by 1848?

The idea of a unified Italy had some support and some potential allies. The educated middle classes and the lesser aristocracy who had seen their influence and power restricted after the 1815 settlement were often waiting and hoping that things would change. In the Papal States and other Italian states, newspapers, books and journals were censored, the middle classes removed from positions of power and absolute rule returned. In reaction many members of the middle classes and minor aristocracy became members of the secret societies, some of these activists pressed for unification.

There was little agreement on how Italy should change within the middle classes – few would have welcomed the radical solution sought by Mazzini and his followers. A unified republic would have meant that the local, state power that the middle classes sought influence over would have been removed to a central power over which they could have little sway. Though a confederation would have been more attractive to some middle-class liberals, the thought of another state like Piedmont dominating the peninsula would have brought the same fears of a centrally unified state. Perhaps a loose confederation headed by the Pope might be more attractive, but in the mid 1840s this seemed unlikely as in the years since 1815 the Papacy had made its suspicion of change and progress very clear.

The power of most of the aristocratic classes in Italy arose out of their positions in their individual states, which they were anxious to maintain. The aristocracy might welcome a confederation which enabled them to keep their power, or perhaps to increase their power over other states, but they would have been very suspicious of the idea of a 'democracy' or a unified republic.

If the idea of a united Italy, in whatever form, was disliked by some, it was completely irrelevant to others. Peasant experiences and attitudes meant that the vast majority were not inspired by the idea of Italy, and gave little thought to a possible future 'Italian' state. As we saw from the actions of Cardinal Ruffo, there might be some potential for the Papacy to lead peasants across the peninsula but we also saw that peasants were, for the most part, concerned with very local issues and the worry of providing for their families.

■ Concluding your enquiry

Now you understand the attitudes that different groups brought to the ideas about Italy's future in the 1840s, complete the table below to estimate the chance of each change actually happening in Italy in the mid-nineteenth century. Explain the reasons for each of your estimates – what makes you think that each idea was more or less likely to be successful?

Type of Change	Percentage chance (each one out of 100%)	Explanation
Unification – a single state of Italy		
Confederation – a group of states led by one of them		
No real change		

As a final step, when your table is complete, make a list of the barriers to change in Italy. In other words, what, in your opinion, would have to be different in order for unification to be more likely than it was in the 1840s?

The 1848 revolutions across Europe

Whole textbooks have been written about the widespread European revolutions of 1848, but unfortunately we only have space to set the scene for the events in Italy. The maps and notes on pages 50–53 aim to help you understand how and where the revolts broke out in Europe, and why the Italian revolts of 1848 were so much more serious than those in the 1820s and 1830s.

The causes of the revolts

Many people across Europe wanted to change the way that their countries were governed, seeking freedom of the press, more democracy and an end to absolutist monarchy. However, as German historians Helge Berger and Mark Spoerer put it (in their article 'Economic Crises and the European Revolutions of 1848' from *The Journal of Economic History, Vol. 61, No. 2,* June 2001):

> While lawyers, publishers, journalists, doctors, and academics were undoubtedly important […] during the 1848 upheavals, they would not have been able to effect revolution on their own. It was the lower classes who provided the 'muscle'.

▽ The revolts and revolutions of 1848 across Europe.

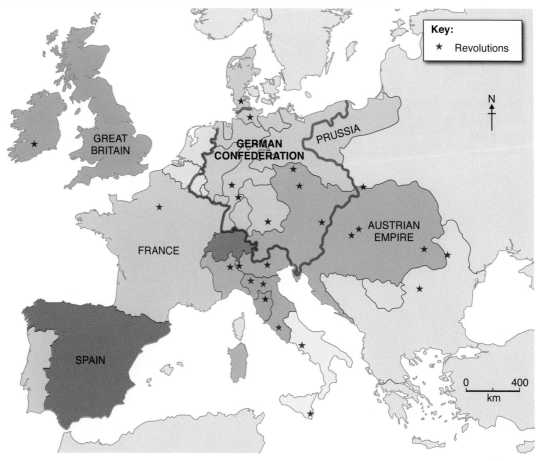

Key:
★   Revolutions

GREAT BRITAIN

GERMAN CONFEDERATION

PRUSSIA

FRANCE

AUSTRIAN EMPIRE

SPAIN

N

0   400
   km

Anger and desperation caused by hunger and disease triggered the 1848 revolutions, which came after two years of bad harvests and waves of diseases like cholera which spread quickly when people have been weakened by hunger. In France and Germany especially, a severe economic depression had brought high unemployment and led to widespread protests.

In Britain a protest movement called the Chartists attempted to take advantage of the revolts across Europe in their campaign for universal male suffrage. A march from Kennington to the Houses of Parliament was planned and it was hoped that 200,000 would take part. The British government stationed tens of thousands of soldiers and recruited 170,000 volunteer special constables to counter this revolutionary threat. In the event only around 20,000 protesters turned out but Chartism kept the prospect of reform alive and most of its aims were eventually acheived.

The main centres of revolution in 1848

France

The last King of France, Louis Philippe, abdicated on the 24 February and a republic was declared after riots and protests in Paris. By November 1848 elections were underway for a new President of the Republic of France, which Louis Napoleon, nephew of Napoleon Bonaparte, won comfortably in December.

Germany

German princes reacted to the revolts which broke out across their states by trying to appease the revolutionaries. Moderate liberals were appointed as ministers, constitutions were promised and representatives were sent to a new 'National Assembly' in Frankfurt, to draw up proposals for a constitution for a united Germany. However, by late 1848 the rulers regained their confidence, replaced the liberal governments with more conservative ministers and abandoned promises of democratic constitutions. The King of Prussia imposed his own, conservative constitution which ensured that his rule was virtually autocratic. By mid 1849 the Frankfurt proposals were complete but were rejected by Prussia and by Austria.

The Austrian Empire

In early March 1848 nationalists in the Hungarian parliament demanded independence. By 13 March, plots and petitions in Vienna boiled over into riots and revolt and Metternich was dismissed as Chancellor in a deal designed to end trouble in Vienna. The news of Metternich's fall caused an eruption of revolutions in Hungary, Bohemia and Italy. Though the Austrian army put down most of the revolts, instability in Hungary continued. In December, Emperor Ferdinand abdicated in favour of his son, Franz Josef. Franz Josef called for help from the Tsar of Russia, who sent in troops to restore Austrian rule in Hungary. By the end of 1849 absolutist rule of the Austrian Emperor had been restored.

The revolutions in Italy, 1848 and 1849

The revolts in 1848 and 1849 were widespread across the Italian peninsula. When King Charles Albert of Piedmont appointed himself figurehead of an Italy that 'would make itself', the revolts seemed to be on the brink of pushing Austria out of her dominant position. However, as we can see from this brief overview, after the initial successes the revolts were ground down when the monarchies began to regain their stability, and when it became clear that the recently 'republican' France would not attempt to spread revolt, or to support 'liberal' or 'radical' rebels in other countries. In Chapter 4 we will look at how this happened in more detail.

Sicily and Naples, 1848

Protests in Sicily escalated in January 1848 into a full scale rebellion, with the aim of breaking away from rule from Naples. The protests also spread to mainland Naples and King Ferdinand II was forced to grant a constitution. The rebels in Sicily still held out for independence, and the new liberal government had to send troops to try to end their revolt. By the spring of 1849 Ferdinand was able to put down the revolt in Sicily and cancel the constitution.

Lombardy, 1848

In what became known as the 'Glorious Five Days' of fighting, Milanese rebels forced the Austrian army out of Milan and into retreat to the border of Lombardy with Venetia. The moderate leaders of the revolt called on King Charles Albert of Piedmont to lead a war of liberation against Austria.

Piedmont, 1848 and 1849

Charles Albert, now the King of Piedmont, was forced by protests to grant a constitution in March 1848, but faced a bigger dilemma when asked by the Milanese revolutionaries to head a war of independence. He dithered and even after declaring war did not strike while the Austrians were in retreat. The Austrians used their military power to punish this indecision, defeating Piedmont twice, in July 1848 at Custoza and March 1849 at Novara.

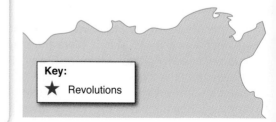

Key:
★ Revolutions

AUSTRIAN EMPIRE

KINGDOM OF THE
TWO SICILIES

★
● Naples

★

N
↑

0   200
        km

Rome, 1849

As you will see on pages 54–55 the Pope raised expectations that he would be a champion of liberal Italy and some even dreamed that he would be the leader of an independent Italian Federation. When he disappointed these hopes, revolution in Rome forced him to flee, and led to the declaration of a Roman Republic. In 1849 France sent troops to Rome to restore the Pope's rule. Garibaldi's defence of the Roman Republic secured his reputation for inspiration and bravery, but even his leadership could not stop Rome falling to French forces in July 1849.

Venice, 1848 and 1849

Venice was one of the first places to see a revolt in 1848 and remained the centre of Italian revolutionary resistance, holding out against the counter-revolutionary forces of Austria for the longest time, until August 1849. Its leader Daniele Manin reluctantly put his faith in Charles Albert in 1848, but continued to resist an Austrian siege after Piedmont's defeat. The siege was ended after cholera and famine forced the republicans to surrender to Austria.

Pope Pius IX – creator of hope and despair

The life of Pius IX can be seen as a tale of two halves. He became Pope in 1846 when he possessed significant powers as ruler of the Papal States and huge moral and religious influence in Europe as head of the Catholic Church. As a result of his early career and views he was hailed as the 'Liberal Pope'. At his death in 1878, he was still leader of the Catholic Church but his temporal power as head of a large and influential state was vanishing. At that point, the Pope's power was now limited to the Vatican City, a tiny fraction of the Papal States with a border that stretches only two miles in perimeter. His liberal reputation had also disappeared because of his staunch opposition to the new, unified Italy.

As a young man his heath was poor. Unable to follow a military career and rejected from the Pope's Noble Guard, he was ordained a priest in 1819 and sent to South America as a missionary. His work there led to him being appointed director of a hospital In Rome, then an Archbishop from 1827. This is when he began to earn the nickname the 'Liberal Pope'. His ideas were shown in 1831 when, as Archbishop of Spoleto, he treated fleeing revolutionaries with leniency. This reputation is partly why his election as Pope in 1846 was such a surprise and why Metternich saw him as a poor choice. In addition he was only 54, young for a Pope.

△ Pius IX, born Giovanni Maria Mastai-Ferretti in 1792, is the longest reigning Pope in history and the first Pope ever to be photographed.

Pius believed that limited reforms were needed. He released political prisoners and allowed thousands of radicals to return from exile. Though it was normal for a new Pope to declare such amnesties, his actions fuelled the belief that he was a liberal. He became a national hero and many began to hope that he could become leader of a united Italy. The Neo-Guelphs had thought for some time that the way forward for Italy was to have a closely knit federation of states that would have a measure of national unity and international recognition through being led by the Pope. Pius also inadvertently encouraged radicals when he suggested a tariff union of Italian states. Unfortunately all his actions did was lead to greater and greater demands. He lost popularity, either because he was too weak or too kind to realise that by giving in to some requests, the people would want more.

Events went too far for Pius in 1848 when Piedmont went to war against Austria. Pius, as the leader of Roman Catholicism, the main religion of Austria, could not take sides, much to the disappointment of his supporters. Then he issued the Allocution (a formal legal statement – see page 63) in which he said that, as leader of all Catholics, he could not support military action against Austria. By doing so he crushed the hopes

PAPAL ALLOCUTION.—SNUFFING OUT MODERN CIVILISATION.

∴ The Pope's allocution justified the construction put upon it in the cartoon.—*April*, 1861.

◁ This cartoon, published in the British magazine *Punch* in 1861, is a satirical comment on the Pope's attitude to the new Kingdom of Italy in 1861. It portrays a richly dressed Pius on tiptoes trying to put out the sun, or 'snuffing out modern civilisation' with a later 1861 Allocution against the new state, and against what Pius saw as the dangers of liberalism and democracy. The cartoon's view is that the Pope is far out of touch, trying to hold back the inevitable modernisation of Italy, represented by the rising sun. This is not surprising coming from a British perspective, where most perceived themselves as part of 'modern civilisation', a key feature of which was a secular government, separated from the Church.

of radicals and neo-Guelphs. Pius had probably never intended to go any further with his 'liberal' reforms, and the revolutions of 1848 underlined to him how potentially dangerous they could be. Pius then fled from Rome with Countess Spaur, a widow thought to have a great deal of influence over him, although little is known about their relationship. He only returned to Rome with help from French troops, who remained in Rome until 1870.

The Allocution changed the attitudes of radicals seeking Italian independence and unity. Mazzini and his followers had always seen the Catholic Church as a barrier to the radical changes that they sought, but after 1849 they became even more anti-clerical, convinced that Pius stood in the way of a united or independent Italy. Pius remained firmly against Italian

unification because he saw it weakening his own temporal power and his influence over Italians. As a result, this once 'Liberal Pope' set himself so firmly against the new Italian government established in 1870 that he published another allocution which called for all Catholics to refuse to participate in elections or government. He even excommunicated King Victor Emmanuel II and his ministers.

Pius remains an important historical figure. He led the Catholic Church through massive changes though his role as an opponent of the new Italian government is arguably more important than the initial hopes for his liberalism. By encouraging Catholics to oppose everything the new Italian state stood for, he weakened the authority of the new Italian state that was already facing many other problems.

4 From hope to despair: Why were revolutionary hopes raised then dashed in 1848 and 1849?

Images of revolution

△ *Liberty Leading the People* was painted in France in the 1830s by Eugène Delacroix, a radical romantic (see page 36) artist. There had been a revolution in Paris in 1830 which saw the fall of the Bourbon Kings and their replacement by Louis Philippe. Louis was known as the 'citizen king' because of his liberal ideals.

◁ *Germania* by Philipp Veit was painted during the 1848 revolutions in Germany. It was displayed in the revolutionary Frankfurt Assembly, a short lived elected German parliament that sat during the revolts in 1848.

In each of these pictures the central figure symbolises its nation – France, Germany and Italy. What are the similarities and differences between these paintings? What might explain the differences?

△ *La Meditazione* was painted in Italy by Francesco Hayez in the years after 1848, and first displayed in Milan in 1850.

Why are these images so different?

You probably noticed that the first two pictures were a lot more 'heroic' and indeed hopeful. Philipp Veit painted *Germania* during the 1848 revolts, when it looked like a united Germany might arise. Germania looks strong, she is well-armed and draped in the national flag and other symbols. France's 'Liberty' is also armed, and she too is shown with national symbols. However, she is not alone, as she leads a group of ordinary Frenchmen in revolt. These both contrast with the figure representing Italy in *La Meditazione*, who is alone, sad and vulnerable. Though you cannot see from this picture, the title of the book on her lap is *A History of Italy*. As a national symbol she seems weak, perhaps in need of protection or help – there is no sense of the optimism or strength that you get in the first two paintings. The first exhibition of this painting took place in 1850, in Milan – the heart of the failed 1848 revolutions in the north of Italy. As you find out what happened in those revolts, you will realise that the message behind this painting would not have been missed.

Paintings like these, while they might not be an accurate record of what actually happened, are excellent sources of evidence for people's attitudes towards these events. In their choice of subject, the symbols that are used, the tone and atmosphere that is created, the artist is trying to say something about their world and what is happening in it. The hope, power and perhaps even dangerous excitement of the people in Delacroix's painting and the confident might of *Germania* contrast strongly with the vulnerability of Hayez's young woman.

Hayez worked into his painting the sadness and desperation of those who wanted change, perhaps even a united Italy, free of foreign dependence, after 1848. Their hopes had ended with not one foreign power controlling or interfering with parts of the peninsula, but two. The revolts and republics of 1848 and 1849 were crushed. Why did people at the time hope that they might succeed, and why did they ultimately fail?

> When you have completed this enquiry, you might want to come back and take a look at *La Meditazione* again. What kinds of imagery might Hayez have used at different points in the revolts?

An outline of the aims of the revolutionaries in Italy in 1848

Before tackling your enquiry for this chapter you need to understand what change would have meant to various groups in Italy in 1848. As the diagram shows, there were many different ways in which Italy might have

No change	= Absolute rulers and dominance of the Italian peninsula by Austria.
Moderate change I	= Constitutional government in each of the different states and increased influence for the middle classes in government.
Moderate change II	= Some kind of confederation or federation where the states share power over some things, but keep the right to decide local matters.
Radical change	= The end of Austrian influence in Italy, the overthrow of kings and dukes and the end of the Pope's temporal powers. Perhaps even a republican government to rule a united Italy.

changed because of the variety of groups there, each with its own opinions and aims.

There were three phases during the revolutions of 1848–49.

1. During the first phase, moderate groups, reluctantly led by **Charles Albert**, the King of Piedmont, initiated attempts to bring change to Italy. However, rather than lead Italy out of Austrian domination, Charles Albert and the other moderate leaders were trying to preserve order in their own states in the face of what looked like a revolutionary tidal wave from Sicily which quickly spread to other parts of Italy.

2. In the second phase, **moderates** gave way to **radical** revolutionaries, with their risings culminating in the 1849 Roman Republic.

3. Finally Austria regained its dominance of the peninsula. Austria, together with France, made sure that the revolutions were defeated.

> **Charles Albert**
> had been the King of Piedmont since 1831. He was the same Charles Albert who had briefly backed the attempted revolt by Piedmontese army officers against Austria in 1821.

> **Moderates** were liberal Italians who wanted change, but change that was not too radical. Liberal ideals included free trade (trade unrestricted by taxes or customs duties) and the freedom of speech (the right to discuss political ideas). Not all liberals believed in all of these things, but many did.
>
> **Radicals** were those who wanted to bring extreme change to Italy, including the removal of kings and their replacement with republics or one united republic for the whole of Italy.

■ **Enquiry Focus:** Why were hopes of revolutionary success raised then dashed in 1848 and 1849?

This enquiry asks you to consider why there was so much excitement and expectation on the part of the revolutionaries in 1848 and secondly, why the revolts were defeated.

1 Take a large piece of paper and draw a line down the middle. On the left, identify reasons why change seemed likely by 1848. On the right, identify the reasons why the revolts failed. Here is a range of possible reasons but if you can think of others then use those too.

the effect of foreign intervention

the impact of Austrian power

the impact of individuals

the impact of different classes/groups of people

religious influences

division and disagreement among rebels

the strength of national sentiments or feelings

the effect of chance or luck

2 Use what you have learned in previous chapters to begin thinking about the question. Use a pencil or sticky notes to place reasons why change seemed likely and why the revolts failed. You can place the same reason on both sides – this tells you that some reasons for expecting change might also help to explain the revolts' failure.

As you read the chapter the tasks will guide you to add to or move the reasons. That's why it's preferable to use pencil or sticky notes – they make improving your answer easier. The tasks will also ask you to make detailed notes about the reasons for the high hopes and, later, failure, so you'll need to collect evidence of the impact of these reasons.

Phase 1: The moderates try to control the revolts

The revolt starts and spreads from Sicily, January to February 1848

In Sicily in January 1848 revolutionaries demanded the restoration of a liberal and democratic constitution that had been put in place in 1812, but revoked when rule from Naples was restored in 1815. They also demanded independence for Sicily from Naples. Despite 5000 soldiers being sent from the mainland and the shelling by the Neapolitan navy, of Palermo, the capital of Sicily, the revolutionaries successfully took over most of the island by April. They then set about electing a parliament, which declared Sicily independent.

The revolution in Sicily then spread to the mainland of the Kingdom of Naples, and King Ferdinand II was forced to grant a constitution to the whole Kingdom of Naples (even though at that point he was not even in control of Sicily). This constitution was very conservative and saved much of the power to make laws and decisions for the king, however it did raise expectations elsewhere in Italy. In February in the Papal States, the Pope also introduced a limited constitution and created an elected **lay** assembly, which could make laws. In February, Charles Albert finally, and very reluctantly, granted a constitution for Piedmont, called the ***Statuto***. Charles Albert had been resisting granting one since the previous year, despite great pressure from moderate and radical protest. The historian Denis Mack Smith tells us that Charles Albert had been furious with Ferdinand II for giving in to pressure from the rebels in Naples, and that he had had to be persuaded not to use force to put down demonstrations demanding a constitution in Piedmont. Events seemed to be moving towards a liberal victory across Italy, especially when the Pope refused to let Austria move troops over his territory to help Ferdinand of Naples put down the revolts in his Kingdom. This confirmed Pius IX's reputation as a liberal Pope.

> **1** Make notes explaining why hopes were raised that the revolutions would be successful.
>
> **2** Review the factors on your piece of paper which explain why hopes were high. Do you want to add any more reasons?

The situation is transformed, February to March 1848

Two events outside the Italian peninsula then inflamed the situation. Firstly, in February there was a revolution in Paris which forced Louis Philippe, the last king of France, to **abdicate**. The French monarchy was replaced with a republic. Following this, riots in Vienna, the capital of Austria, forced the resignation on 13 March, of Metternich – the Chancellor who had done so much to keep Austria's position as the leading power in Europe. The situation seemed now to be completely transformed. Might

lay
Refers to something or someone that is not directly part of the clergy of the Catholic Church. Laypersons are ordinary Catholics, not priests or cardinals. Pius IX's 'lay' assembly was made up of ordinary people elected to pass laws and to advise the Pope

The *Statuto*
This was a constitution for Piedmont, though Charles Albert disliked the idea of having one so much that he refused to call it a constitution, using the term 'The Statute' or *Statuto* in Italian

abdicate
When a king or queen steps down from their position as monarch

the leaders of the new French Republic lend help to those wanting change in Italy? Would Austria still be able to control Italy now that Metternich was gone? Many in Italy saw opportunities for change, and tried to take them.

That change did seem to be taking place in the wake of the revolutions in Sicily and Naples. The middle and aristocratic classes in Milan in Lombardy had been protesting since January at their lack of influence in Lombardy-Venetia. In mid-March they began a new and clever protest, designed to cut the revenue that Austria received in taxes from the region. The Milanese stopped smoking and gambling because both activities involved paying large amounts of taxes. The historian Martin Clark tells us that Austrian soldiers retaliated by smoking ostentatiously in the streets and were attacked by gangs of grumpy, nicotine-withdrawn Milanese. Six people were killed in the trouble.

This tension escalated after the news reached Milan that Metternich had resigned. Between 18 and 22 March five days of furious fighting in the streets led to the defeat and withdrawal of the Austrian army. The Austrian General Radetsky wrote in a dispatch to the Austrian court in Vienna on 22 March, 'It is the most frightful decision of my life, but I can no longer hold Milan. The whole country is in revolt'. After some argument between moderates (who feared a republic of Lombardy) and the radicals led by Carlo Cattaneo (who wanted a republic of Lombardy), a moderate provisional government was formed, the radicals agreeing to seek help from the Piedmontese monarchy. The new government, therefore, asked Charles Albert, the King of Piedmont, to defend them against the Austrians. Casati, **Podestà** of Milan, representing moderate opinion, was afraid that if Charles Albert did not take charge, radical republicans would take control of the revolts.

This mood of change and hope also took root in Venice, where on 22 March a Venetian republic was declared, led by Daniele Manin. Manin was a republican and a Venetian nationalist. At first he wanted an independent Venice and took the title of 'Doge'. This had been the title of the head of the Republic of Venice, which had existed from the seventh century until it was conquered by Napoleon in 1797. However, Manin was also a pragmatist and saw that Venice could not stand alone for long against Austria. Eventually he too asked Charles Albert for help, but this was after a long delay and a furious debate between radicals and moderates in the city. In the meantime, revolutionary troops from Naples (under the control of General Pepe) and from the Papal States (under General Durando) marched north to help Lombardy and Venice in a war that seemed to offer the chance of independence from Austria.

So, by the end of March 1848 it seemed that change really was coming to Italy. The Austrians had been pushed out of Milan by a popular revolution which had then declared support for a 'kingdom of upper Italy' to be led by Charles Albert of Piedmont. The Austrians were distracted by revolts across their territory. Soldiers and volunteers were travelling from the south of the Italian peninsula to offer their support to the King of Piedmont in his fight against Austrian domination.

Austria seemed to be on the back foot. It had lost the leadership of Metternich, its troops had withdrawn to fortresses on the border with Lombardy, and almost all the large states of Italy were in open revolt

podestà
A term used in medieval and early modern Italy that meant a local mayor or governor. Casati took the title as head of the provisional government in Milan following the retreat of the Austrians from the city

against Austrian rule. To add insult to injury even the Papacy seemed to be encouraging hopes of Italian liberation.

---

1 Make notes explaining:

    a) why hopes were raised that the revolutions would be successful

    b) any weaknesses that were already apparent in the revolutionary movements.

2 Review the factors on your piece of paper which explain why hopes were high. Do you want to add any more reasons?

Charles Albert makes his move, eventually, March 1848

The hopes of the revolutionaries were high but Charles Albert of Piedmont did not immediately support the revolts in Milan. In the words of the historian, Denis Mack Smith, he 'waited for four vital days until he was satisfied that the war was likely to succeed and to be in Piedmontese interests'. Only then did Charles Albert declare that 'Italy will make herself' and mobilised his forces against the Austrians. 'Piedmontese interests' meant that, in return for defending the revolts, Piedmont would take control of Lombardy. What he meant by 'Italy will make itself' was that the war should be won without the help of the new Republic of France. This was because Charles Albert was afraid of a republic being formed in Lombardy and of a republican revolution taking place in his own country. This made him suspicious of help from the new French republic. Consequently, Charles Albert did not send his troops into Lombardy until the 22 March, by which time Radetsky and his army had escaped to the safety of the fortresses of the Quadrilateral, four strong defences on the border with Venetia, from where they could regain their strength.

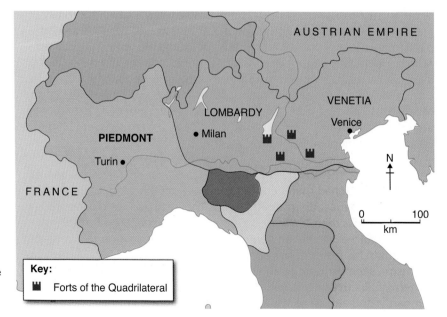

▷ The states of northern Italy in revolt from March 1848, showing Piedmont, Lombardy, Venetia, the forts of the Quadrilateral and the capital cities of Turin, Milan and Venice.

Phase 2: The moderates are defeated and the radicals take centre stage

The Papal Allocution, April 1848

On 29 April 1848 the Pope delivered what the historian Christopher Duggan describes as a 'body blow' to the national movement. Pope Pius IX issued 'the **Allocution**' in which he made clear that:

- he didn't want to lead an Italian Federation
- the Austrians were the rightful rulers of Lombardy and Venetia
- the kings and dukes were the rightful rulers of the other states and should be obeyed.

Pope Pius made this declaration *against* the war with Austria after he lost control of General Durando, the commander of his own Papal army. Against the Pope's orders, Durando had taken troops north to fight the Austrians. The historian Denis Mack Smith describes the Allocution as a 'bombshell' and suggests that the Pope had finally realised that a 'liberal' Pope could not be an absolute ruler of the Papal States. When he did, Pius IX had to make a sharp U-turn and make it clear to Austria and France that he was not encouraging the revolts against Austria.

According to another historian, Martin Clark, the Allocution made moderates and liberals choose between their religious and political views, that is between loyalty to the Church and to the revolution. Many of the revolutionaries chose the latter and fought on for their political beliefs. Though the Allocution had removed the Papal seal of approval for the war, and some soldiers probably did return home as instructed despite the news being suppressed in Venetia, the practical effect on the fighting in the north was minimal.

> **Allocution**
> A speech made by a Pope on an important issue, which is then published and distributed throughout the Catholic Church. It is used to make the Church's views clear to ordinary members and, during the period we are studying, to send clear messages and signals to other rulers

The defeat of Charles Albert, July 1848

Charles Albert's aim was to expand Piedmont. For Mack Smith this was the main reason for the failure of the 1848 revolutions. It meant that the Piedmontese couldn't fight alongside the republicans (because Charles Albert was opposed to republicanism), and that he couldn't accept the help of the **Neo-Guelphists** who wanted the Pope to rule an Italian Federation. Therefore, he relied on Piedmontese troops and ignored the need to keep the support of both radicals and moderates in the fight against Austria.

> Look back to Chapter 3 to find out more on **Neo-Guelphists** – these were people such as Gioberti who hoped that the Pope would rule a united, federal Italy.

Charles Albert's hopes for expansion also meant that he waited until he was sure of gaining Venetia as well as Lombardy to take military action against Austria. In the long period between 22 March and June 1848 little action was taken against the Austrians. Whilst Radetsky was on the back foot in the five days of March 1848, Charles Albert wobbled and did not take the fight to the Austrian troops who were in retreat. Instead of being pushed out of Lombardy and Venetia all together, Radetsky was allowed to retreat to the Quadrilateral fortresses. This gave him the opportunity to build his army up to 70,000 by the summer of 1848, compared to Piedmont's 20–30,000.

It was clear that Charles Albert had overestimated his own military prowess and that of his army. Piedmont was defeated in July 1848 at the Battle of Custoza where the Italians were outnumbered three to two. Charles Albert made this overestimation not once, but twice when in March 1849 he attempted to re-start the war. This time the Piedmontese forces slightly outnumbered the Austrians, but even so, Charles Albert's army was smashed again by troops under the command of Radetsky, at the Battle of Novara on 23 March 1849.

▷ The Austrians end the revolts of northern Italy in 1848 and 1849.

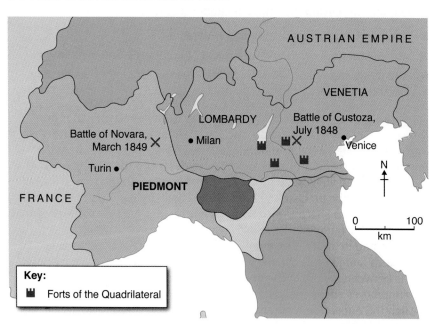

Continue to review and add to your notes.

64

Radical revolutionaries take the initiative, August to November 1848

Through the first half of 1848 the moderates led by Charles Albert of Piedmont and Casati, Podestà of Milan, had been at the head of the attempt to liberate Italy from Austrian rule. As their attempts failed, more radical revolutionaries tried to bring change to Italy. In Venice, Daniele Manin resumed his leadership of the Venetian Republic, which held out against a siege by Austrian forces until August 1849, even though Charles Albert had been defeated at Custoza and the Austrian army had re-taken most of the state of Venetia.

Radicals also developed a hatred of Pope Pius IX, following what they saw as his betrayal in publishing the Allocution against the war with Austria. After the defeat of Piedmont in July 1848, many radicals who had left Rome to fight the Austrians in the north returned home. The Pope was alarmed that the city was filling up with armed radicals and appointed Count Pellegrino Rossi as his prime minister to deal with this threat. Rossi hated radical ideas and introduced unpopular measures to control the people of Rome. According to the historian Harry Hearder, many radicals feared that he was planning to abolish the 'lay' assembly and constitution brought in by Pius IX earlier that year. As a result of these fears, Rossi was stabbed to death on 15 November 1848 as he walked to the assembly in Rome. Pope Pius fled Rome in fear of his life a week later. In February 1849, the parliament of Rome decided to draw up a new constitution for Rome and declared a new republic, taking the dramatic step of announcing the end of the Pope's temporal power.

See page 25 for information on temporal power.

Did the ideas of the radicals bring more hope than those of the moderates?

If we read the following extracts, one from Charles Albert's *Statuto*, and the other from the Decree issued by the assembly of the Roman Republic, we can see the similarities and differences between the ideas that were driving the moderate and more radical revolutionaries of 1848–49.

Extract from the Piedmontese *Statuto*, 4 March 1848

Article 2: The state is governed by a representative monarchical government. The throne is hereditary …
Article 5: To the King alone belongs the executive power …
Article 6: The King appoints to all of the offices of the state, and makes the necessary decrees and regulations for the execution of the laws.

Extract from the Decree of the Roman Assembly, 8 February 1849

Article 1: Papacy has fallen, in fact as in law, from the temporal throne of the Roman State.
Article 2: The Pope shall enjoy all guarantees necessary for the exercise of his spiritual power.
Article 3: The Government of the Roman State is to be a democracy and shall be known as the Roman Republic.
Article 4: The Roman Republic shall maintain relations with the rest of Italy as required by a common nationality.

As you can see, the two documents are quite different. The *Statuto* reserves many powers for the King, whereas the Decree makes it quite clear that the Pope, as monarch of Rome, has lost all his earthly (temporal) powers. In fact, the *Statuto* states that the government of Piedmont will be 'monarchical', and the Decree that the government of Rome will be a democracy. If you noticed that the Decree also puts Rome in the context of Italy, then you have spotted something important – the *Statuto* treats Piedmont as a state alone, whereas the Decree makes a point of mentioning Rome's place in the rest of Italy.

▷ This engraving by an unnamed artist, published in the *Illustrated London News* in 1849, shows a group of Garibaldi's men during the French assault. It gives a sense of the distrust that some in Britain felt towards the radical republicans who had taken over Rome.

We can see from these differences that the radicals were offering a much bolder vision of a democratic Rome, as part of an Italy with a 'common nationality'. The moderate *Statuto* kept much of the power for the King of Piedmont, but under the Decree, power is supposed to come from the people. These ideas attracted radicals to the defence of the City of Rome. After the republic was declared in February 1849, Rome was ruled by a **triumvirate**, the most memorable of whom was Mazzini himself. The new republican government introduced a number of laws that, although they only lasted as long as the republic, showed how radical it was. They abolished the *macinato*, the tax on grinding corn, which the peasants hated paying. Press censorship was brought to an end, and land that had been owned by the Church was also seized by the new government.

As well as Mazzini, the triumvirate (group of three) was Carlo Armellini and Aurelio Saffi.

Summary: Why were the hopes of the revolutionaries raised so high?

There were some very powerful reasons why the hopes of those wanting change were raised so high in 1848. There was a much wider range of Italian society involved in 1848 than in earlier revolts. Peasants in Sicily and Naples, alongside the middle classes in the army, had forced Ferdinand to grant a constitution. The middle classes in Piedmont had done the same, and the revolution was being led by the King of Piedmont and seemed to be supported, to some extent, by the Pope in Rome. In Venice the ordinary citizens supported a revolt led by the middle classes and in Milan such citizens had forced the Austrians from the city and into retreat.

There was also a wider spread of Italian states involved than in earlier revolts, from Sicily right up the peninsula to Piedmont, and the revolutionaries seemed to be working better together than they had in previous revolts – soldiers and volunteers from Naples, Rome, Piedmont, Milan and Venice were prepared to fight alongside each other. As well as these immediate reasons for high hopes was the growth in the previous decade of the idea of 'Italy'. As we saw in Chapter 3, many Italians had been discussing the possibility of the Pope or of Piedmont leading Italy away from Austrian domination. Now it seemed that Piedmont, with the support of the Papacy might actually achieve independence from the Austrian Empire.

Another crucial element was the unusual weakness in Austria's position due to wide-spread revolts across the empire. In Hungary, Austria eventually had to call for help from Russia to restore order. Revolts and riots had even spread to the capital and Metternich had been forced to resign. More generally there was the influence of events across Europe. The French had overthrown their king and declared a republic. Germans were clamouring for a united Germany. No wonder the hopes of some in Italy were raised so high.

> ■ Continue to add to and review your notes as you did earlier in this chapter.

Phase 3: Austria regains her balance and France helps to defeat the radicals

As we have seen, the revolts of 1848 and 1849 came in waves, from Sicily up to Naples and then to Lombardy, Venetia and Piedmont and finally to Rome. Each wave was defeated individually but by a set of common forces. This section explains how these defeats came about.

The defeat of Sicilian rebels, May to September 1848

Ferdinand II had initially agreed to a constitution for Naples, following the spread of the Sicilian revolts to the Neapolitan mainland. However, the moderate democrats who had pressured Ferdinand to grant a constitution were worried by the number of peasant revolts that followed across the southern kingdom. The radical democrats were also afraid that Ferdinand was preparing to overturn the constitution and so rioted in Naples on 15 May. This, ironically, gave Ferdinand the excuse that he needed to use his army to dismiss his elected assembly and to start to regain absolute control. By September 1848 Ferdinand had cancelled the constitution and re-appointed his conservative ministers. Ferdinand then offered to rule Sicily through a **viceroy**, and give the island its own parliament and ministers. The Sicilian rebels rejected this offer, so in March 1849 Ferdinand's army invaded Sicily, with orders to take any steps necessary to regain control of the island. By mid-April Sicily had been re-conquered.

viceroy
A ruler appointed by the king to rule on his behalf

The double defeat and abdication of Charles Albert

As we have seen, Charles Albert's army, ill prepared and badly trained, was defeated by the Austrians at the Battle of Custoza in July 1848. An armistice lasted until March 1849, while the Great Powers made half-hearted attempts to negotiate a settlement between Piedmont and Austria. The election of Louis Napoleon as president of the new French Republic in December 1848 seems to have encouraged Charles Albert to believe that the French would now intervene on Piedmont's side. Perhaps Charles Albert hoped that under the leadership of the heir of Napoleon Bonaparte, France would again try to unseat Austria as the dominant power in Italy. Charles Albert therefore attempted war once more in March 1849. However, the French did not intervene on Piedmont's side and Charles Albert was immediately defeated, at the Battle of Novara (see page 64). Charles Albert then abdicated, leaving his son Victor Emmanuel II as the new king. Having defeated Piedmont twice, Austrian forces could then turn their attention to the revolts in the Papal States.

The defeat of the Roman Republic, February to June 1849

Mazzini (the idealist nationalist we met in Chapter 3) arrived in Rome in February 1849. Following the defeat of Piedmont at Novara, he was put in charge of the Roman Republic. The Republic was surrounded by enemies. From the south, Ferdinand II of Naples had regained his absolute powers and his army was preparing to help with the restoration of the Pope in Rome. From the north, Austrian troops entered the Papal States and in early May 1849 set about ending the revolts in northern cities such as Ferrara and Bologna. Meanwhile, another threat to the Roman Republic came from France.

The declaration of the French Republic in 1848 had been followed by the election of an assembly. France was overwhelmingly Catholic and the assembly was therefore conservative and supported the Pope in his appeal for help against the Roman rebels. Louis Napoleon, elected as President in December 1848, had good reason to think that the Roman republic would fail, and so intervened against Mazzini and the republic. This enabled him to win not only the approval of French Catholics, but also to reassure the other powers of Europe that he was not an immediate threat to the balance of power. By sending troops to Rome in April 1849 Louis Napoleon re-assured the other powers that he was not a radical republican. He also won some military glory for France and was able to gain a little influence for France in Italian affairs.

See page 10 if you need reminding of what *Risorgimento* means.

However, French military glory was not easily won. The defence of the Roman Republic entered the legends of the *Risorgimento*. The volunteer army of Rome, under the brilliant leadership of Giuseppe Garibaldi, first defeated the army of France, then the army of Naples, before returning to face a re-enforced army of 40,000 French troops. Rome was finally captured by the French, but only in June 1849 when, following weeks of fighting and great loss on both sides, Garibaldi led a column in retreat

◁ *Garibaldi carrying his dying Anita* painted in 1864 by Pietro Bauvier, an Italian artist. This picture captures the idea of sacrifice that became part of Garibaldi's appeal as a symbol of Italian unity.

out of the city and across the Apennine mountains, while Mazzini slipped away using a false passport. Garibaldi hoped to carry on the struggle through a campaign of guerrilla warfare, and appealed for followers, saying 'I offer hunger, thirst, forced marches, battles and death!' Four thousand revolutionaries left with him, but found that the peasants of the Roman countryside would not support them. Their campaign soon fizzled out and Garibaldi's wife Anita was killed in the long march across Italy. In the years afterwards the Roman Republic, and its heroic defence became a powerful symbol of Italian nationalism.

The defeat of the Republic of Venice

The last of the republics of 1848–49 to fall was that of Venice, under the leadership of Daniele Manin. Not made of the usual stuff of heroes, Manin suffered from long bouts of a depressive illness, which led him to crippling self-doubt on occasion. Despite this and his lack of experience, Manin was a popular leader with the Venetian citizens and they remained loyal to him throughout the siege of Venice by Austrian forces at sea and on land. The historian Paul Ginsborg puts this popularity down to the tradition of pride that the people of Venice had in the city's independence. Manin embodied this pride by taking on the role of 'Doge' (see page 61).

Despite the faith of his people, Manin was a pragmatic leader, and realised that the Austrians would win the siege eventually. However, he hoped that there might be a negotiation between Venice and the Austrians. This might give the city some sort of independence or autonomy from Austria, especially if the British supported him. However, the British representative in Venice, Clinton Dawkins, disliked Manin, doubted his abilities and thought that, in continuing to resist the Austrians, Manin was deceiving himself as well as the people of Venice. Dawkins' conservative views made him pro-Austrian and anti-republican and he fed stories of chaos and anarchy in Venice back to Palmerston, the British Foreign Minister, in London. Britain did not therefore pressure the Austrians into reaching a settlement and Austria was given a free hand to continue the siege.

The siege of Venice saw what the historian Jonathon Keates, in his book *The siege of Venice*, describes as 'history's earliest recorded attempt at aerial bombardment', which ended with 'inglorious failure' when the Austrians launched scores of small balloons, each one loaded with explosives. According to Keates, when the wind direction changed and the bombs exploded over the Austrians' lines there were cheers of 'Bravo!' and 'Buon appetito!' from the watching Venetians. However, despite the intervention of the wind on that occasion, and continued resistance from the Venetians, the Austrian siege continued. Starvation and cholera eventually ground down morale inside the city and Venice finally surrendered on 22 August.

■ Take another look at your paper. Do you need to move or add any more reasons for hope or reasons for failure? Once you are happy with their position, finish your notes about the effect that each factor had on both the hopes of the revolutionaries and the eventual outcome of the revolts.

■ Concluding your enquiry

1 Look again at your notes and at the position of your sticky notes on your piece of paper. Make sure that you're happy that the order of your sticky notes reflects your thoughts on their comparative importance.

2 For each reason on each side of your piece of paper write two sentences. The first should explain why you think that was an important reason why the revolutionaries' hopes were raised or dashed. The second, why you think that reason was more or less important (depending on where you placed it) than the others. These sentences would then make a great essay plan, which you would need to complete with evidence to back up your points. You might even want to write this essay.

3 As a final step, take all the sticky notes off the piece of paper. Where would an Italian radical defeated in 1848 place those notes? Which would he place at the top and bottom as the most important reason why the revolutionaries had great hopes, and the most important reason for their hopes being dashed? What about a recent historian? Which notes would they place in these important positions?

How has the judgement of historians changed?

At the start of this chapter we saw, in Hayez's *La Meditazione*, a woman representing Italy gazing resentfully out of the picture after reading her own history. This painting was exhibited in 1850 and was the first interpretation of the events of 1848 and 1849. Her message is clear – Italy had been betrayed. For the radicals and republicans who had taken part in the revolts, the sense of betrayal was indeed clear. We can see this from a letter written by Mazzini to an English friend on 6 August 1849, which exclaimed that 'Rome has fallen! It is a great crime and a great error. The crime belongs entirely to France; the error to civilised Europe and especially to your England'.

In the decades following the unification of Italy historians also tended to see the 1848–49 revolutions as having been betrayed. In *Garibaldi's Defence of the Roman Republic* (1907) the historian G.M. Trevelyan said that 'As some 12,000 of his subjects were taking to the field [the Pope] cut the ground from under their feet by the famous 'Allocution'. From that day onwards he had forfeited the sympathy of all good Italians'.

However, as we have seen before, historians writing in the twentieth century have shifted their focus from the deeds and failures of great men and instead have looked to other factors to explain the events of 1848. For Lucy Riall the strength of the Austrians was the main reason for the failures of 1848–49, 'In April 1849 [after Novara], Austrian domination of the Italian peninsula was reaffirmed once more'. Riall also argues that the revolutionaries' leaders were not up to the job, a theme taken up by Mack Smith, who describes Charles Albert's call to arms, *Italia fara da se* (Italy will make herself) as 'absurd', and says that his military skills 'were negligible'. Darby agrees that 'Charles Albert was inadequate to the task, an incompetent general and a poor leader'.

The fact that Italy could not 'make herself' was also a theme taken up by those writing at the time, and afterwards. Writing in May 1849, Benitto Ricasoli, a liberal politician who eventually became Prime Minister of Italy, said that 'Italy cannot possibly free herself without outside help', a view echoed by Woolf writing in 1979 of the 'isolation and vulnerability of the republicans at Rome and Venice' and the failure of Britain to intervene to prevent Austria regaining control in Italy. Woolf hints that there was an unspoken agreement between the Great Powers that the revolutionaries should not be allowed to succeed, and that this agreement broke down in the years after 1849, something that we will turn to in the following chapters.

'Reading' political cartoons

Cartoons are excellent sources for historians. They can help us understand what happened but they tell us more about how people felt about events and ideas. This is because cartoons show the artist's opinions – how they saw their world and the events that they witnessed, read or heard about. This in turn helps us understand why people acted the way they did.

Because political cartoons are about opinion, we have to learn to read them in a particular way and place them in **context**. Our aim should always to be to understand the point of view of the cartoonist and how and why he or she came to that view. Fortunately, cartoonists help us to grasp their point of view by using a common set of techniques.

context
What was happening at the time the cartoon was drawn – the events, people and ideas that were active in people's minds

Captions and labels – If an object is supposed to represent something in the real world, like a treaty, battle, country or idea, the object will often have a label naming it.

Speech bubbles – As in modern day comic books, cartoonists often used speech bubbles, sometimes looking like scrolls of paper or banners.

Sizes of people and objects – This is often used to make us compare things. A big person next to a small person might indicate that one is more powerful than another.

Facial expressions and posture – Cartoonists use faces when trying to persuade us, because they know that we will focus on a face in a cartoon. Anger, cruelty, honour, wisdom, drunkenness, greed and other emotions will be presented and used to persuade us to agree with the cartoonist's point of view.

Distortion or caricature – If a person is being criticised then they will be made to look less attractive. On the other hand, ideas and people that the cartoonist wants us to support or be attracted to will be made to look handsome or beautiful. Italy, for instance, is often represented as a beautiful woman who needs protection.

Shading and colour – Most of the cartoons that we will see are black and white ink sketches, though a few may be in colour. Shade and colour are used in similar ways. Sometimes light and dark moves our eye around the picture. An important, brave, kind or wise person might be shown in a pool of light or in rays of light from a sun. Dark shadows and corners often hide cruel, or cunning evil-doers or symbols of oppression.

Arrangement of objects – Like the use of dark and shade, sometimes the position of objects is used to help the cartoonist get his or her view across. Important things might be above those less important. Items being pressed or squashed represent oppression. Something that is overshadowing or threatening another is often put at the top of a picture.

Symbols in cartoons about Italian unification

Cartoonists often use symbols to represent people, ideas, countries, and events. They choose these symbols carefully to express an opinion about whatever is being represented. Sometimes these are obvious, but often you need to know the context, or understand the meaning of the symbol itself.

Animals

These should be easy to read, but often the meaning depends on how an **animal** is drawn. For instance, a lion usually means strength and bravery, and a snake betrayal and cunning. But, what would it mean if a country had been drawn as a weak lion?

Hats

Cartoonists love hats. They can be used to show what job a person does, or what their views are or station in life. The size of a hat can make a person seem silly. The angle can make someone seem rushed, anxious or weak. Hats are often symbols in their own right. Obviously a crown is a symbol of rule or monarchy and the Pope's multi-layered crown shows his temporal and spiritual authority. The 'Phrygian cap', or **liberty cap** became a symbol of revolution and republicanism, but also of progress and freedom generally. It was used in cartoons sometimes as a symbol of hope for change and sometimes as one of fear of revolution.

Religious symbols

Statues, candles, altars, light from the heavens, **keys of Saint Peter** and other religious symbols are used. Sometimes the cartoonist wants to create a vision of purity, strength or that God approves of a person or event. Sometimes religious symbols are used to criticise, especially if the cartoonist is critical of the Pope.

Boots

Stivali means boot in Italian. A boot is often used to represent Italy or the peninsula. The state of the boot, what it looks like, where it is, will help you understand the point the cartoonist is trying to get across.

Punch

A great number of the cartoons from this period come from the British satirical magazine *Punch*. *Punch* was not a magazine as we would imagine it. It contained news stories and comment pieces that were supposed to inform and amuse its readers. *Punch* represented a conservative British view of the world; it was suspicious of radicalism, the Papacy and particularly of the French, Britain's traditional enemy.

Sometimes each **animal** refers to a country – Britain is often shown as a lion, bears often refer to Russia, and eagles to Austria. Oddly France is rarely shown as an animal but by a drawing of Napoleon III (his large nose is often caricatured).

The **liberty cap** – sometimes called a 'Phrygian cap' – refers to a special kind of felt cap that Roman slaves wore when they had achieved their freedom.

The **Keys of St Peter** is a symbol of two crossed keys, which represent the Papacy. They are St Peter's keys to heaven.

One cartoon about unification

If we look at a cartoon that you might not have seen before and which refers to events that we have not yet covered in detail, we can practise our skills of reading a cartoon and trying to understand the point of view that the cartoonist hoped to persuade people to agree with.

Context

This image was published in Britain in *Punch* magazine in 1859. It was published at the end of the 1859 war, when it had been agreed that a new Kingdom of Italy would be created, but without Venice, Rome or the Two Sicilies. The kingdom was created with the help of the French Army. The French had made it clear that they would protect the Pope's position and did not want the South to be part of this new kingdom.

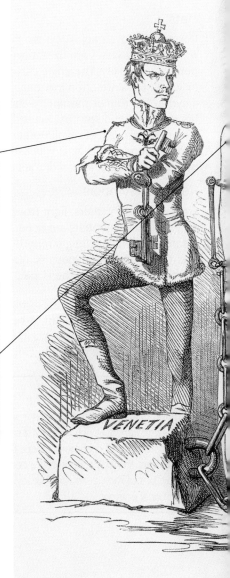

Austria

This figure represents Austria, which we can see from the crown and the small symbol of the bird on its tunic. The fact that this person has the keys which control Venetia, on which he proudly holds his foot, also helps us to work out that this is indeed Austria. We can also see that Austria has a cruel, or perhaps proud look on its face as it looks towards the central figure.

Italy

This figure is the most important of the cartoon, which we can tell because it is in the middle right over the caption 'FREE ITALY (?)'. This woman therefore represents Italy, but she is not really free, and she looks unhappy as we can see from her expression. She holds a staff with a Phrygian cap, but she cannot wear it because another figure is holding a Papal crown over her eyes – which means she cannot be free because of the Pope, who is being supported by the last figure. Other details, such as her dress and bare feet suggest that Italy is weak and vulnerable.

VENETIA

FRE

(?)

This is also a ruler – and if we look at the large nose and exaggerated moustache we can quickly tell that this figure represents Napoleon III and France. France's threat to protect the Pope means that Italy cannot be free, because unification cannot take place. Though we cannot see Napoleon's expression, he is a faintly silly figure, with a pot belly and an ornate jacket covered in medals. This tells us that the British cartoonist wants to ridicule him.

Looking at these three figures helps us to explain the caption's question mark. 'Free Italy' is not a statement, it is a question. Italy's freedom is questionable because she is unhappily shackled to Austria through Venetia as Austria still controlled that part of Italy. She is under the influence of the Pope and the French. As we will find out, very quickly after this cartoon was printed it became clear that French control over Italy was much weaker than is suggested in this cartoon. This doesn't make the cartoon wrong, or bad evidence. On the contrary, it makes it great evidence of the attitude that some in Britain held towards the events of 1859, and their fear that France was becoming dominant in Italy. This is a good point to remember. Bias and subjectivity can make a source extremely useful for historians, as such sources can tell us a great deal about the attitudes and beliefs of the people who made or wrote them.

5 How was Italy united under the leadership of Piedmont between 1848 and 1870?

As you've read in the last chapter, the 1840s did not end well for those who hoped to see a unified Italy. Charles Albert, the King of Piedmont, abdicated after the humiliation of two military defeats at Austria's hands. The new king, Victor Emmanuel II, had to tread carefully to avoid upsetting Austria. The revolutions in the other states across Italy – in Sicily, and in the rest of the Kingdom of Naples, Tuscany, Venetia, the Papal States – had all failed. Each saw the restoration of their monarchs, with the help of foreign troops from Austria or France. Austria's domination of Italy had been confirmed, and the ideas of Mazzini, Balbo and of Gioberti seemed to have been entirely discredited. It seemed that Italy was not going to 'make itself', either by popular revolution or under the leadership of the King of Piedmont or of the Pope in Rome.

However, as we will see in Chapters 6–8, Piedmont's position improved, even as Austria's isolation increased. By 1859 Piedmont and France had allied in a war that was the first major stage in the creation of a single kingdom of Italy. As a result Austria gave up the rule of Lombardy to Piedmont and Piedmont took control of Tuscany, Parma, Modena and much of the Papal States. The following year, 1860, a seemingly miraculous campaign by Garibaldi ended with the defeat of Naples and the annexation of most of the south of Italy by the new Kingdom of Italy. In 1866, following a short war with Austria, Venetia was added to the kingdom and in 1870 Rome was also captured. Unification was complete.

> ■ **Enquiry Focus:** How was Italy united under the leadership of Piedmont between 1848 and 1870?
>
> Take an A3 piece of paper and use the account on the following pages to construct a timeline of the events of the unification of Italy from 1848–70. We have split the account up into key stages to help you. Each stage has a map so that you can see how Italy changed over the period. Do not write lots of notes as you will cover these events again in the following chapters. Instead, focus on recording the key events, their dates and briefly note down the major reasons for changes.

The development of Piedmont as Italy's leading state, 1849–58

After Charles Albert abdicated in 1849, his son Victor Emanuel became the new King of Piedmont and negotiated a peace treaty with Austria. The treaty was not a very harsh one, since the Austrians were eager to avoid further revolts in Piedmont. Piedmont did pay damages and some of her fortresses were occupied by Austrian troops but Austria insisted that Victor Emanuel keep the *Statuto*, in an effort to maintain his support among Piedmont's moderates and middle classes.

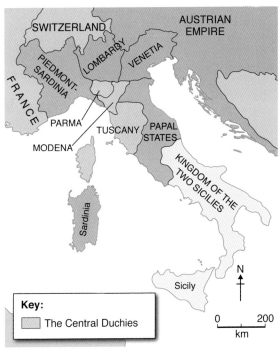

△ Italy in 1858, just before the 1859 War of Independence.

The parliament and the limited free-speech allowed by the *Statuto* helped Piedmont to become an attractive refuge during the 1850s for moderate nationalists from around the peninsula who found themselves unwelcome in their home states. The economic, political and social reforms put in place by the energetic Prime Minister, **Cavour**, further raised Piedmont's reputation as the most liberal state in Italy. Piedmont's economy grew quickly as these reforms took hold, and Cavour invested the increase in tax revenue in Piedmont's transport infrastructure and her military. Cavour's knowledge of how the British parliament worked, and his willingness to seek political alliances with both the left wing and right wing of politics enabled him to stay in power and also gave him the reputation of being a powerful political figure.

Piedmont's position as Italy's leading state was further emphasised by her role in the **Crimean War** (1854–56). Britain and especially France were hoping to bring Austria into their alliance against Russia and so decided to bring Piedmont into the alliance too, so that Austria would not fear a Piedmontese threat while putting pressure on the Russians. Cavour could see the advantages in negotiating a deal with Britain and France but Victor Emanuel was very enthusiastic, and bullied Cavour and the Piedmontese Parliament into declaring war on Russia without securing any definitive advantage for Piedmont in return. Victor Emmanuel wanted to take part because he thought the Crimean War would give Piedmont a chance to prove the strength of her military. In the one battle in which it took part, Piedmont's army did well. After the war, the question of Italy was briefly discussed at the Congress of Paris of 1856, but by the end of the conference it seemed unlikely that either Britain or France would do very much to remove Austria from Italy.

Of much more significance was the effect that Austria's role in the Crimean War had on the balance of power across Europe. Until then Russia had been Austria's strongest ally. During the 1848–49 revolts it had been Russia who came to Austria's aid by using her army to end the revolts in

For more information on **Cavour** see the insight on pages 102–103.

For more on the **Crimean War**, see pages 93–95.

Austria's Hungarian provinces while Austria put down revolts across Italy. However, Russia's attitude changed because it felt betrayed by Austria's role in the Crimean War and from 1856 onwards Austria could no longer rely on Russian help. Furthermore, Prussia was beginning to challenge Austria's dominant position across the states of Germany. France too was starting to challenge Austria's position in Italy, as Louis Napoleon III, having declared himself Emperor in 1852, was looking for ways to displace Austria as the dominant power in Europe.

The Second War of Independence, 1858–59

It was an alliance with France that gave Piedmont a chance to expand her borders at Austria's expense. Following an **attempt by Orsini**, an Italian radical, in January 1858 to assassinate Napoleon, the French Emperor began to see that Italy might be an ideal place to start to reduce Austria's power. He met Cavour at the French spa town of Plombières for secret negotiations and to plan a war that would see Piedmont take control of Lombardy, Venetia and other parts of northern Italy. Napoleon hoped that this new Kingdom of Northern Italy would be under French influence, and that this would severely weaken Austria's hold on the rest of the Peninsula. In order to disguise an aggressive and cynical attack on Austria, France and Piedmont had to make it look as if their action was a response to Austrian aggression. This would be hard to achieve.

France and Piedmont spent much of 1858 trying to goad Austria into war. By the spring of 1859 it seemed as if Napoleon was frustrated with their failure to do so, and Austria sensed that Piedmont was losing her ally. This caused Austria to make a fateful mistake. Austria issued an ultimatum threatening Piedmont with war unless the Piedmontese army was moved away from the border with Lombardy. This made Austria look like the aggressor and gave France and Piedmont an excuse to declare war.

In the war of 1859 Austria could not stand up to the combined forces of France and Piedmont, though Piedmont's contribution in soldiers was not as great as Cavour had promised. Garibaldi's troops did win a small victory in May, but the important battles at Magenta and Solferino in June were fought mainly by French forces and were **costly victories** for France.

The costs of the 1859 war for France

The British and Prussians were both alarmed by French actions in 1859, due to the prospect of France becoming the dominant power in Italy. However, the real cost was in blood. At Magenta the French lost 650 men, over 3500 were wounded, and at Solferino they suffered 2000 dead, and over 4000 wounded. (See Chapter 6 for more details.)

In the rest of the Italian states, by June 1859, there were demonstrations and revolts in Tuscany, Modena, Parma and in parts of the Papal States, started or encouraged by Cavour's allies. However, initially they seemed to have little impact, because of Napoleon III's change of tactics. In July 1859, Louis Napoleon III, concerned by the threat of the Prussians joining the

---

■ What were the key events in this period? Note them down, along with the dates, on your timeline. Also list the factors responsible for major developments towards possible unification.

The war of 1859 is known as the 'Second War of Independence' in Italy. The 1848 war between Piedmont and Austria is known as the 'First War of Independence'.

It might seem surprising that an assassination **attempt by Orsini**, an Italian nationalist, would persuade Napoleon to intervene in Italy. You will understand why after studying Chapter 6.

war on Austria's side, and worried that the Papacy was threatened by the actions of Cavour's allies, decided to negotiate peace with the Emperor of Austria. Piedmont was not even told about this Treaty of Villafranca until it was signed. Villafranca did grant Lombardy to Piedmont, but also ordered the restoration of the **rulers** of Parma, Modena and of Papal rule in the northern Papal States. Cavour resigned in a rage, furious that a chance to dislodge Austria from Italy altogether had been missed.

The **rulers** of Parma, Modena and Tuscany fled their duchies in 1859, and there were revolts in some cities of Romagna in the Papal States. These areas were then controlled by committees of local liberals or members of the National Society (see Chapter 7).

NAPOLEON III ET L'EMPEREUR D'AUTRICHE SE PRÉSENTANT LES PRINCIPAUX OFFICIERS DE LEURS ÉTATS-MAJOR, APRÈS LA CONFÉRENCE DE VILLAFRANCA.

△ Napoleon, Emperor of France and Franz Joseph, Emperor of Austria meet at Villafranca, 1859. You will notice that there are only two sides in negotiation – the Piedmontese were not invited and were informed of the decisions made without having the chance to influence them.

◁ Piedmont's annexation of Lombardy as set out in the Treaty of Villafranca.

■ What were the key events of this Second War of Independence? Note them down, along with the dates on your timeline. Also list the factors responsible for major developments towards possible unification.

The annexation of the Central Duchies, and Garibaldi's Expedition of the Thousand, June 1859–October 1860

Despite the Treaty of Villafranca however, further change was on the way. By the end of 1859 it was clear that the Treaty was not going to be implemented. The rulers of the Central Duchies were not restored. Cavour's allies had organised **plebiscites** which returned large votes in favour of annexation by Piedmont. Napoleon saw that, unless he acted, France would gain little for the sacrifices made during the 1859 war, because Piedmont was becoming too strong for France to dominate in the way that Napoleon had intended. In December 1859, he published a pamphlet which suggested that the Pope would not regain control over the northern Papal States. Cavour (who had been appointed Prime Minister again) negotiated a new deal with France in the Treaty of Turin, which saw Piedmont gain the Central Duchies and the northern Papal States, in return for paying the French costs of the 1859 war, and giving Nice and Savoy to France.

plebiscite

A vote or referendum by the population of a place, taken in order to get people's opinion on an important matter. Historically they have often been used to confirm something already decided, and have often been rigged

▷ The Kingdom of Italy December 1859, following the Treaty of Turin.

Cavour's concessions were not popular. While Savoy was a French-speaking province of Piedmont, Nice was very Italian in character and the birthplace of Garibaldi. Garibaldi and other nationalists objected to the annexation of Nice by France, and in 1860 he planned a revolt in Nice designed to stop France taking over. Garibaldi was instead persuaded, by Francesco Crispi, an Italian nationalist from Sicily, to use the volunteer troops that he had gathered and instead take them to the island, which was again in revolt against rule from Naples. Crispi argued that Sicily was much more likely to rise up in support of Garibaldi than Nice, and Garibaldi eventually agreed.

This campaign of 'the Thousand' has become one of the key stories of the *Risorgimento*. **Garibaldi's** badly armed forces won a series of victories that seemed miraculous, conquering first Sicily and then the Neapolitan mainland. By September 1860 it looked as if Garibaldi might invade the Papal States from the south. However, Cavour knew that if the Pope's rule of Rome itself was threatened this might cause France or Austria to intervene to protect him, leading to war for the new state of Italy against either or both of her powerful neighbours. Therefore, Cavour sent the Piedmontese army into the Papal States, defeating the Pope's army and meeting Garibaldi's forces before they could attack Rome itself. At Teano in October 1860, King Victor Emanuel II met and shook hands with Garibaldi. Garibaldi gave control of the south to the King and returned to his home on the island of Caprera. This left the Pope in control of the city of Rome and its surrounding territory which was not part of the new Kingdom of Italy.

△ The Kingdom of Italy 1860, following Garibaldi's Expedition of the Thousand.

■ What were the key events during 1860? Note them down, along with the dates on your timeline. Don't forget to list the factors responsible for major developments towards possible unification.

Piedmontisation, the Brigands' War and Venice, 1860–66

See Chapter 8 for more details of **Garibaldi's** campaign.

Having created an Italian state, it had to be made to work. Though some called for a new constitution, the Piedmontese *Statuto* was applied across Italy, as eventually were Piedmont's criminal and civil laws as well as its education system. A system of local government was also put in place, which saw **prefects** being appointed by Victor Emanuel's government in Turin. This 'Piedmontisation' was resented by many across Italy, especially in the south. An especially powerful symbol of this process was Victor Emanuel's insistence on continuing to be called 'Victor Emanuel II' which connected him to the Piedmontese dynasty, rather than taking the title of Victor Emanuel I of Italy.

Resentment in the old Kingdom of Naples at conscription into the Italian Army and high taxes imposed from the north, boiled over into revolt and almost into civil war. Politicians from the north blamed this trouble on the low morals of those in the south. The 'Brigands' War' as it came to be known, held down 120,000 Italian troops and caused the deaths of thousands by the time it was over in 1865. Even after this date travelling in the south was dangerous, and robberies common.

prefects
These are governors, or representatives of the government in a province. In Italy these prefects were appointed by the King and his ministers and had a lot of power over matters such as censorship, the police and justice

△ Garibaldi, after his arrest at Aspromonte. Garibaldi was shot in his ankle, an injury which never fully healed.

The unexpected death of Cavour in 1861, probably from malaria, meant that Italy lacked his political and economic skills at a crucial time. Those that followed him could not command the same support in the Italian parliament or control the King in the way that Cavour had done. By 1870 the prime minister had been replaced eight times.

While Italy's politics lacked leadership, the Papacy still bitterly opposed unification. Stung by the experiences of 1848 and 1859, Pius IX issued a Syllabus of Errors, a document which condemned all the 'mistakes' of progress and liberalism that the new Italy stood for. The opposition of the Pope did not have a great deal of practical effect, but it was a symbol of the lack of support that the new Kingdom had among many 'Italians'. While the Pope objected, and while he still had the support of the French, Rome could not become part of the Kingdom.

Garibaldi twice tried to settle the matter of Rome by military force. In 1862 he gathered a second army of volunteers. It is unclear whether this was done with the support of Prime Minister Urbano Rattazzi, but when it became clear that the French would not allow Italy to take control of Rome, the Italian army was used to arrest Garibaldi at Aspromonte on the very southern tip of Italy.

The pride of Italy was further dented by defeat in the 1866 Austro–Prussian War. Prussia, keen to press her advantage over a weakened Austria, and with the intention of dominating the states of Germany, declared war on Austria in June 1866. Austria offered to give Venetia to Italy in order to keep her out of the war, but Prime Minister General Alfonso La Màrmora wanted a great victory against Austria in which Italians could strengthen their national pride, and therefore Italy joined forces with Prussia against Austria. In reality the war was a disaster for the Italians who were beaten by the Austrian army and navy, despite the large investments that had been made in Italy's armed forces since 1861. Austria was beaten by the Prussians, but Austria refused to give Venetia directly to Italy because Austria had defeated Italy so conclusively. Instead, in order to make it clear that she had not been defeated by the upstart new state, Austria granted the province to France, which then handed it to Italy.

■ What were the key events of the period 1860–66? Note them down, along with the dates on your timeline. Add to your list of factors responsible for unification.

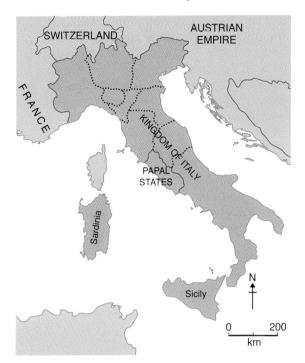

◁ The Kingdom of Italy in 1866, following the Prussian War.

Garibaldi, the Pope and Rome, 1866–70

Problems still dogged the new state in the second half of the 1860s. It seemed to many that the joining of Venice to Italy had not been achieved through a war of liberation, but instead after military humiliation. The national debt was growing quickly in order to pay for the creation of the new state, the wars of 1859 and of 1866 and the suppression of the 'brigands' of the south. A particularly aggressive southern revolt in 1866 was only put down when troops could be moved from the north after the end of the Austro–Prussian War.

Garibaldi made one final attempt to take Rome for Italy in 1867. However, when the Romans failed to rise up against Papal rule and in support of Garibaldi, and when the French made it clear that they would not allow the Pope to be threatened, Victor Emanuel ordered the arrest of Garibaldi. Napoleon III sent his troops back to Rome to protect the Pope. It looked as if it would be many years before Rome would become the capital of a united Italy.

△ Bismarck, the Chief Minister of Prussia, and Napoleon, Emperor of France, talking together after the Battle of Sedan in 1870. Napoleon had been captured and spent the rest of his life in exile from France in London. Without Napoleon's protection, the Pope's temporal power was very vulnerable.

The situation changed very rapidly in 1870, when France was goaded into a war with Prussia. At the Battle of Sedan at the end of August 1870, Napoleon III was captured and a revolt in Paris ended his reign. In the meantime French troops had been withdrawn from Rome, but Italian forces held off from invading the city until France had been defeated. When news of Napoleon's capture reached Italy an attempt was made to create an uprising inside Rome in favour of unification. When this was, again, a failure, Italian troops used artillery to open a breach in Rome's walls and the city was forcibly joined to the rest of Italy.

Victor Emanuel died in 1878, and in 1880 a huge memorial in Rome – the *Vittorio* – was commissioned in honour of the first King of Italy. The memorial was completed in 1935 and was very controversial. Many Romans call it the *zuppa inglese* because it looks like this Italian desert of layers of cake and custard piled on top of each other.

■ Add the new events to your timeline, with their dates. Are there any more factors that caused unification that you can add to your list?

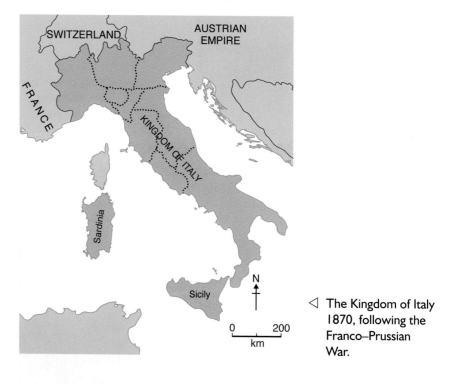

◁ The Kingdom of Italy 1870, following the Franco–Prussian War.

■ **Concluding your enquiry**

Now you have a timeline, and an overview of events, take one more look at the events leading up to the unification of Italy. Use your timeline to come up with a spider diagram summarising the factors that you have identified. Pay careful attention to the links between factors – make sure that in your notes you describe how these links worked to help cause unification.

The rest of this book

You will be referring to this list of factors and your timeline as you read the second half of this book. Chapters 6–9 analyse the period in more depth from different perspectives, so please don't worry if we cover the same event more than once. We will read about the diplomatic changes which made the unification of Italy possible, as well as looking at how the development of Piedmont made it the leading state in the process of unification. We shall also learn about the role of Garibaldi as well as other leaders such as Cavour and Victor Emanuel. Finally, we shall consider whether Italian unification was a success and how well the Italian state did in the years following 1870.

Why are there so few photographs of the events in Italy in this book?

When this book starts, in 1815, photography hadn't been invented. It wasn't until 1839 that two different photographic methods were first announced, one developed by Louis Daguerre, the other by William Henry Fox Talbot.

Even then, and until the 1870s, the uses of photography were limited. One reason was that exposure times of several seconds were too slow to record fast-moving events and bustling crowds. In addition, one method very commonly used from the 1850s (the wet collodian process) incorporated fragile glass negatives which had to be prepared, used and developed, all within a few minutes.

As a result much of the photography before the mid-1870s was studio-based portraiture or, if outdoors, people were posed in rather stiff tableaux, as in the picture of Garibaldi on page 82. Accordingly these photos lacked the drama and variety of the artists' reconstruction drawings that newspaper-readers were familiar with. In Italy, the classical ruins were the most photographed subject because of the increasing tourist market – and because the buildings never moved!

From the 1870s the styles and types of photographs changed quickly with improvements in cameras, their lenses and photographic techniques allowing 'street' photography, 'event' photography, 'amateur' photography and photo-journalism (as we'd call them today) to develop. However, that was all after this book ends!

Napoleon III and Victor Emmanuel II

Emperor Napoleon III and King Victor Emmanuel II both had a considerable influence on the events you'll read about in the remaining chapters. You will find studying their influence all the more interesting if you know something of their background and character, which are covered in this insight section.

Napoleon III

Following the defeat of his uncle at Waterloo in 1815, Louis Napoleon spent his early life in exile. He and his mother lived in Rome, Switzerland, England, Bavaria and Italy. Nonetheless, Napoleon was well educated and lived a privileged life, meeting many powerful and influential figures.

Italy had a particular influence on Louis Napoleon. He spent his late teenage years in Rome, at a time when he was beginning to think about politics and the position of France in the balance of European power. His uncle's victories in Italy and his desire to follow in Bonaparte's footsteps may also have played a part in his interest. When he reached adulthood, Napoleon and his brother returned to Italy and joined the Carbonari, one of the secret societies who worked to undermine the power of the Austrians in Italy. He took part in the failed revolutions of 1830, before fleeing with his brother to France from Austrian reprisals. His brother's death from measles then seems to have spurred Louis Napoleon's ambition, and he began preparing to become leader of France. He went through military training and started writing about his belief that France should be ruled as a monarchy very much on the Napoleonic model.

Louis Napoleon was exiled from France in 1836 after an attempt to overthrow the King. In 1848, revolution in France established a Republic. To many people's surprise, Napoleon's name carried enough weight to win election to the office of president of the new republic in December 1848. In 1852, when his presidency would otherwise have ended, he staged a coup d'état and took power on the 48th anniversary of his uncle's coronation as Emperor of France.

△ Napoleon III, was born Louis Napoleon in 1808 in Paris during the reign of his uncle, Napoleon Bonaparte. Against all odds and predictions, Louis Napoleon himself became Emperor Napoleon III of France in 1852. However, in another echo of his uncle's life he died in exile, following the defeat of France by Prussia in 1870.

Victor Emmanuel II

Victor Emmanuel had a military upbringing, and his love of army life and of battle was apparent throughout his reign. He was never comfortable with the constitutional monarchy he inherited following the abdication of his father in 1849. Though he wished for a more autocratic arrangement, Victor Emmanuel found that he needed parliament and, increasingly, that he needed Cavour to help re-build the army and the country's finances following the disasters of 1848–49.

During the 1850s the King contented himself with using the **prerogative powers** remaining in his hands to create opportunities to win glory for Piedmont and himself. The most obvious way to do this was through war. Victor Emmanuel was convinced of his ability as a military strategist and longed for a chance to prove his abilities to the rest of Europe.

His manners were rough and his strong language shocked diplomats in France and Britain during visits in 1855; at the same time he enjoyed causing diplomatic problems by telling the British what the French really thought of them, and the French how the British saw them as a 'parcel of adventurers'. The historian Denis Mack Smith tells us that Victor Emmanuel tried to set Queen Victoria against her Prime Minister, Palmerston, and offered his hand in marriage to Princess Mary, the Queen's cousin. She tactfully turned him down, but wrote to her father that Victor Emmanuel was 'thoroughly coarse minded'. His behaviour was so bad that Cavour threatened to return to Piedmont without the King, if he did not stop.

Following Cavour's death, Victor Emmanuel continued to intrigue in international politics. He planned revolts in the Hungarian Kingdom during the 1860s. He was hoping to start another war, so that the new Italian Kingdom could expand its borders. He also had ambitions to place his son on the throne of Greece, and there is evidence that he was behind Garibaldi's attempts to capture Rome in 1862 and 1867. Victor Emmanuel died in 1878 and his son Umberto I struggled to fill the place left by his charismatic but flawed father.

△ Some of Victor Emmanuel's brusque character comes across in this bust made by the Italian sculptor Emilio Marsali. The King had to be persuaded to trim his extravagant moustaches before a diplomatic trip to France and Britain in 1855.

The king's **prerogative powers** were his right to decide on important powers such as: declarations of war; choice of ministers and when to call or dismiss parliament.

6 Why did Austria lose her grip on Italy by 1860?

We have seen in the first chapters of this book how unlikely the unification of Italy was between 1815 and 1848. We learned that the revolts in the 1820s and 1830s failed to bring any real change to any of the Italian states, and that, following the failed 1848 revolutions, Austria's position of power and influence across the peninsula had been confirmed. Austria's strength and control over Italy was evident in the abdication of King Charles Albert of Piedmont, the French suppression of the Republic of Rome and the surrender of the Republic of Venice to Austria in 1849.

However, as we saw in **Chapter 5**, within ten years of these events Austria had been driven from Lombardy and Piedmont was on the verge of annexing not only Lombardy, but also Parma, Modena, Tuscany and a good deal of Papal territory. The focus of this chapter is on how Austria lost her grip on Italy by 1860 when this had seemed so unlikely in 1848. In the next chapter we'll look at how changes in Piedmont contributed to this process but here we will look at the European-wide events and circumstances which gave Piedmont the chance to challenge Austria's hold on Italy.

Take a look at this diagram, which represents the situation in 1815:

If, during this analytical chapter you need a reminder of the sequence of events, turn to **Chapter 5** for a summary.

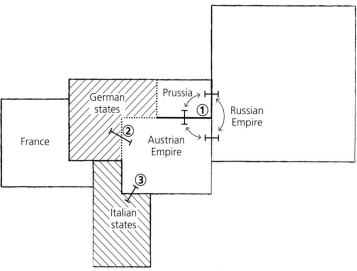

① The Troppau Protocol. Signed in 1820 by Austria, Prussia and Russia, which gave each country the right and perhaps even the duty to use their armies to prevent revolution in each others' territories.

② Austria held the position of 'president' of the German Confederation, which included Prussia.

③ Austria dominated the Italian peninsula by direct rule (as in the case of Lombardy and Venetia) or by military force – which she had used between 1815 and 1848 to maintain the status quo.

△ Austria's dominance of Italy and central importance in Europe 1815–54.

You will see that Austria is firmly at the centre of the 1815 settlement which was designed to make sure that no one country (especially France) had too much power. Italy was dominated by Austria so that France could not use Italy as a way of dominating the rest of Europe. You can see that Germany is shaded in a similar way to Italy because Germany too was a collection of kingdoms and dukedoms, split up to stop either Prussia or Austria gaining too much power over the rest of the continent. The German states were allies with Austria, with Prussia or sometimes both.

France was also firmly contained by this situation. After the defeat of Napoleon in 1815 France had to accept new limits. The rulers of France accepted this, and whilst they would have liked to increase the role and prestige of France, they didn't want to risk another war so soon after the defeat of Napoleon in 1815. Prussia, Austria and Russia were all absolute monarchies. They had a common interest in preventing change which might risk their positions in Europe.

Now let's look at the situation between 1856 and 1860:

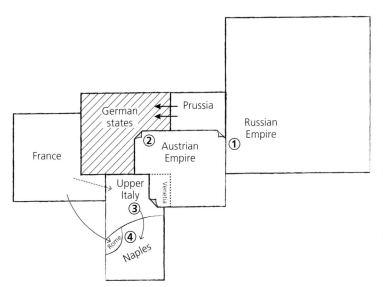

① Austria's decision in 1854 to support the British and French in the Crimean War against Russia was seen by the Russians as a betrayal. From 1856 Russia sought opportunities to weaken her old ally Austria.

② Prussia was pressing for more and more influence in Germany, and Austria was increasingly economically isolated by Prussia's free trade agreements with the other German states.

③ In 1859 France and Piedmont fought a war against Austria which created a new Kingdom in upper Italy, forced Austria from Lombardy and removed her influence from the central duchies.

④ Austria could do little when Garibaldi's volunteers attacked Sicily and Naples and then threatened the Pope in Rome.

△ **Austria's isolation from 1856.**

We can see now that France was attempting to gain influence in Italy, whilst Prussia was doing the same in Germany. Austria had lost her very close relationship with Russia and within six years would be at war with Prussia; who would dominate Germany. As a result Austria was losing her grip on Italy. A united Italy was created in the window of opportunity created by this shift in the balance of power in Europe.

■ **Enquiry Focus:** Why did Austria lose her grip on Italy by 1860?

This diagram shows the different factors that led to Austria's isolation and the breaking of the 1815 settlement.

Why did Austria lose its grip on Italy?

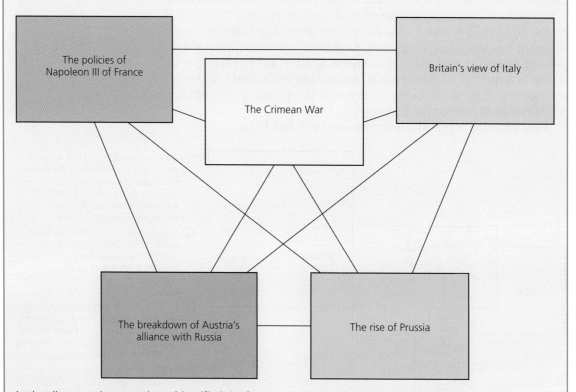

In the diagram above we have identified the factors that caused Austria to lose her grip and how they linked together. Your task in this enquiry is to explain the links between the factors. You will make notes about how each factor helped to break Austria's grip on Italy but you will also note down suggestions about how each factor worked with others to end Austria's dominance. At the end of the chapter you will create a final diagram like this explaining the links.

Having read Chapter 5, you may already be able to suggest how some of these links worked. Therefore, draw a copy of this diagram and note down possible explanations. As you read this chapter you can build up this diagram and change your mind about the links if necessary.

The policies of Napoleon III of France

Louis Napoleon, the nephew of Napoleon Bonaparte, was elected President of the Republic of France in December 1848, following a revolution earlier that year which had toppled King Louis Philippe from his throne. In 1852 Louis Napoleon proclaimed himself Emperor Napoleon III. The end of monarchy in France and the seizure of power by a member of the Bonaparte family turned out to be a key moment for Austria and, because of this, for Italy.

The Vienna Settlement, which Austria had defended since 1815, had the key aim of preventing France from dominating Europe in the way that she had during the reign of Napoleon Bonaparte. However, in the 1850s the strong possibility of conflict between France and Austria developed, because Napoleon III's regime wanted to increase the power of France and needed to remain popular with its people. An aggressive and successful foreign policy was one way in which Napoleon III could achieve both these aims.

But Napoleon III had to tread carefully. He knew that there was a risk that the other powers of Europe might invade France in order to restore Louis Philippe, or simply to remove another Bonaparte from power. Therefore, Napoleon took an early opportunity to reassure the rest of Europe that he would not support radical republicans, when he sent French troops to Rome in 1849 to end the Roman Republic. At the same time by putting a dent in Austria's dominance over Italy and by presenting France as the protector of the Papacy, this increased the prestige of Napoleon at home.

France's re-invigorated ambitions in Europe and especially in Italy added a sense of uncertainty to Austria's position. By 1854 this pushed Austria to abandon its Russian alliance in order to avoid conflict with France over the Crimean War (see page 93). This, in turn, added to Austria's isolation after the war ended in 1856.

> You will find more detail about **Louis Napoleon** in the Insight section on pages 86–87.

PUNCH, OR THE LONDON CHARIVARI.—February 19, 1859.

L'Empire c'est la paix

THE FRENCH PORCUPINE.
He may be an Inoffensive Animal, but he Don't Look like it.

◁ This cartoon was published in the British magazine *Punch* in 1859, just before the war with Austria. It presents Louis Napoleon as a porcupine protected by guns, bayonets and swords. He is saying 'L'Empire, c'est la paix', which was a saying of Napoleon I meaning 'the Empire is peace'. This suggests that in Britain some feared that this Napoleon III would be as aggressive as his uncle, Napoleon I.

A chance event in January 1858 enabled Napoleon to exploit Austria's growing isolation and further disrupt the 1815 settlement that had prevented France from increasing her power. On 14 January, while the Emperor was travelling to the opera in Paris, an Italian radical, Felice Orsini along with other conspirators, threw three bombs at the imperial carriage. Eight people were killed and more than 150 injured. Miraculously, the Emperor and his wife were both unharmed. Orsini was arrested, tried and sentenced to death. He wrote movingly to Napoleon from prison to explain his actions:

> Let me remind Your Majesty that Italians, including my own father, cheerfully shed their blood for Napoleon the Great, and they were loyal to the end. Let me also remind you that neither Europe or your Majesty can expect tranquillity until Italy is free.

For more on the meeting at **Plombières**, see page 112.

Napoleon saw that this could be an opportunity to explain and persuade the French public that a war in Italy might be in France's interests. Furthermore, Piedmont's embarrassment that the plot had been hatched in her territory gave the French Emperor a moral weight to negotiate an alliance with Piedmont in France's favour. Napoleon therefore saw an opportunity to move against Austria, and he allowed Orsini's letter to be published to help make the case for French intervention in Italy. Napoleon's next step, in July 1858, was to attend a secret meeting with Count Cavour, the Prime Minister of Piedmont, at **Plombières** in France. At this meeting, Napoleon and Cavour plotted to provoke a war with Austria. Napoleon III then sent his nephew, Prince Jerome, to meet the Russian Tsar to make sure that Russia would not interfere with France's plans to defeat the Austrians. When the French and Piedmontese successfully provoked Austria into war in 1859, Russia did play an important part in helping to tie up Austrian troops.

The Battle of **Magenta** was so destructive, so bloody that it gave its name to the deep, red colour of blood on the battlefield, known after as 'magenta'.

At the Battle of **Solferino**, Henry Dunant, a Swiss man, was so horrified by the suffering of the dying that he was inspired to start a charity to aid those hurt by war. This is now known as 'The Red Cross', and carries out humanitarian work in war-zones across the world.

French troops were vital to the success of the campaign against Austria in 1859. Cavour had hoped, and indeed had promised to provide a large army to match France's contribution of 120,000 men. In reality Piedmont could only muster 60,000. The army was further hampered by their lack of maps, supplies and proper planning (these problems had also plagued Piedmontese forces in the First War of Independence in 1848). Victor Emmanuel insisted on leading the troops personally, despite the fact that he really wasn't very good at it. Christopher Duggan describes the King's fondness for 'out-dated' cavalry charges, for instance. As a result of these various difficulties the Piedmontese army actually arrived too late to take part in the first major battle of the war, at **Magenta** on 4 June. The second major battle, at **Solferino** on 24 June was even bloodier than Magenta, though this time Piedmontese forces did fight side-by-side with the French. The Austrians withdrew to their Quadrilateral fortresses (the same fortresses they had used in their retreat in 1848, and which are shown on the map on page 62) on the border with Venetia. However, around this time Victor Emmanuel realised that the siege artillery which the Piedmontese had promised to provide had been forgotten, and was still in Piedmont.

As we will see in the next chapter, while these battles were being fought, Piedmontese agents and their allies in the **National Society** had started or were taking control of revolutions in the other states of central Italy. When it appeared that Cavour was trying to annex Tuscany (which was not part of the Plombières Agreement) this and the bloody cost of the battles increased Napoleon's fears that Piedmont was gaining too much at the expense of France.

Napoleon knew that the next stage of the war, removing Austria from its fortified positions, would cost even more. This, and the threat of the Prussians intervening on Austria's side, led Napoleon to negotiate with Austria and to the signing of the Treaty of Villafranca in August 1859. This treaty ended the war, left Venetia in the hands of Austria and demanded that Piedmont restore the rulers of the Central Duchies.

However, by December 1859 Napoleon realised that the Piedmontese had cemented their control over central Italy. Unless he negotiated again with Cavour, France would have gained nothing for its part in the war. When he demanded Nice and Savoy, two areas of Piedmontese territory on the French side of the Alps, Cavour agreed, as the cost of French support for the annexation of Parma, Modena, Tuscany and the Romagna. The Treaty of Turin was signed in March 1860 and France took possession of Nice and Savoy from the Piedmontese following plebiscites in both areas which seemed to show public enthusiasm for annexation by France.

The **National Society** was a group of former radical nationalists which formed in Turin in 1857, and which decided to work with the Piedmontese monarchy in order to try to force the Austrians from Italy. We will look at its activities in Chapter 7.

■ Make notes on this section, using these questions to guide you:
- Why was France such a pre-occupation for Austria?
- How did Napoleon III change France's relationship with Austria?
- How did Napoleon III contribute to Austria's isolation?
- How did Napoleon III help to bring about the creation of a Kingdom of Italy in 1861?

You may also be ready to start noting possible links between this factor and others in the diagram. Don't worry if you change your mind as you read on – there will be a chance at the end to review your explanations of the links.

The Crimean War, 1854–56

Like most wars, the **Crimean War** had a variety of causes. Britain feared Russian expansion into territory controlled by the Ottoman Empire because this expansion might threaten Britain's control of India. Austria also feared Russian expansion because much of the Austrian Empire was made up of Slavic people, from the same ethnic group as Russians. There was also the risk that Russian expansion might encourage the Slavs in its Empire to ask Russia for help or protection and could lead to conflict. France saw an opportunity to weaken Russia, to disrupt the 1815 settlement which had contained French ambitions, and to gain an alliance with Britain (Napoleon III's view was that his uncle's biggest failure was that he never managed to ally with Britain).

The **Crimean War** was fought between Russia on one side and Britain and France on the other.

What started as a dispute over who should control and protect the holy sites in present day Israel and Palestine, became a crisis when Russia invaded the Ottoman Empire in July 1853 to test the reaction of the other powers. Britain and France demanded Russia's withdrawal and sent a fleet to back up their threat. Russia did withdraw but only after the British and French deadline had passed. By this time public opinion in Britain and France, and Napoleon's eagerness for a military alliance with Britain, led them to invade Russia in the Crimean peninsula. It was hoped that a quick victory would lead to Russia accepting that she could not expand into Ottoman territory.

▷ Where the Crimean War was fought.

Both Russia on one side and Britain and France on the other wanted Austria as an ally. According to the historian R. F. Trager:

> Austria was confronted with a stark and unwanted choice over the Crimean War. If Austria were to side with Russia, she would risk the enmity of the Western Powers [Britain and France], and revolution in Italy, increasing her dependence on Russia. If Austria sided with the West, she might alienate her powerful neighbour [Russia].

The Austrians tried hard to avoid the war, and when their attempts at peace-making failed they still hesitated to support either side. But they were forced to declare their hand eventually and joined the alliance of Britain and France against their traditional ally, Russia. As we will see below, this decision had a profound effect on Austria's relations with Russia.

The Crimean War also affected Piedmont's standing within Italy and her relations with Britain and France. Napoleon III and Britain courted Piedmont as an ally in the war with Russia. They did not expect the Piedmontese army to play an important part against Russia but instead wanted Piedmont as an ally to re-assure Austria that she would not face a revolt led by Piedmont in Italy while Austria's armies were fighting in the Crimea.

Cavour could see some advantages in becoming involved in the war and allying with Austria if a good deal could be negotiated. King Victor Emanuel II was very keen to take the opportunity to send Piedmontese troops to fight. As we will see in Chapter 7, Victor Emanuel was so determined that Piedmont should take part in the Crimean War that Cavour was forced to hastily agree to Piedmont sending her army.

Piedmont's troops performed well in the one major battle in which they took part, the Battle of Chernaya on 16 August 1855, and this cemented its reputation as the only state in Italy with a capable army. Piedmont was also allowed a place at the Congress of Paris that met in 1856 to agree a treaty to end the war. Italy was discussed, but only briefly, and only in relation to the need for reform in the Papal and Neapolitan government. However, no moves towards unification were discussed or suggested in the formal meetings. As we will see, Cavour made several ham-fisted attempts to form anti-Austrian alliances with Britain and France but these came to nothing. One of the important legacies of the war, though, was that Cavour and Napoleon III did meet and contact between them continued in the years after 1856, notably at Plombières in 1858.

■ Make notes on this section, using these questions to guide you:
- Why did Austria hesitate over who to support in the Crimean War?
- What effect did the Crimean War have on Austria's position in Europe?
- What effect did the Crimean War have on Piedmont and Italy?

More links between this factor and some of the others should be becoming more obvious. Note down any explanation of these links that you can.

The breakdown of Austria's alliance with Russia

Before the 1850s Austria and Russia had developed a very close alliance. Russia, along with Prussia, had been keen supporters of Metternich's policy of intervening in states where revolution threatened to topple the rulers. They had signed the Troppau Protocol of 1820 which gave each country the authority and indeed the duty to suppress revolutionaries in other countries who threatened the status quo. This agreement had been used to end the revolutions in Italy in 1820–21 and 1831. In 1848 Russia had, at Austria's request, sent her army into Austria's Hungarian provinces in order to end a revolt there and to prevent Hungary gaining her independence. The two empires were so close that in 1853 the Tsar of Russia, when asked about Austria's views on the impending Crimean crisis, said 'When I speak of Russia, I speak of Austria as well. What suits the one, suits the other. Our interests as regards Turkey are perfectly identical'.

However, by 1853 when this remark was made, the Austrians were feeling less confident about the future of their alliance with Russia. Their relations had come under strain as a consequence of the slow **break-up of the Ottoman Empire**, a mutual neighbour. Austria had its eye on gaining land in the Ottoman provinces nearest to it while Russia was also interested in obtaining some of the crumbling empire's territory, which might bring the two into conflict. When war became imminent in 1853, the Russian Tsar and his advisors told themselves at first that Austria's failure to support Russia could be explained by Austria's worries over possible French aggression and the loss of influence in Italy, but that Austria would soon join the Russian side. However, when it became clear in January 1854 that Austria would side with Britain and France against Russia, the Tsar wrote to the Austrian Emperor accusing him of treachery. When Russia was eventually defeated, he believed that Austria's 'betrayal' had contributed to this defeat.

The impact on Austria of this break with the Russians was enormous, but can be boiled down to two key issues.

Firstly, the Troppau Protocol was dead – Russia no longer supported the Austrians in their use of military might to end revolutions in Austrian territory or **sphere of influence** and this clearly included Italy. One example of this change is that Russia provided subtle support for France and Piedmont during their 1859 war against Austria. As we have seen on page 92, before attempting to provoke war with Austria, Napoleon III decided to check that Austria's traditional ally, Russia, would not come to its aid. The outcome of the meeting between Prince Jerome of France and Tsar Alexander II is strong evidence of Russia's changed relations with Austria. Russia agreed to use its influence to try to prevent Prussia from joining in the war on Austria's side. Russia also moved troops to the border with the Austrian Empire, forcing the Austrians to keep some of their forces on that border in case the Russians attacked and so away from the fighting in Italy.

The second consequence of the break between Austria and Russia was that it quickened the pace of Austria's isolation and loss of influence within Germany, which aided the rise of Prussian power. As we will see, the rise of Prussia contributed a great deal to the steps in the later stages of unification that saw Italy gain control over Venice and win Rome as her capital.

The **Ottoman Empire** was controlled from Turkey which at the height of its power had conquered large areas of North Africa, the Middle East as well as the Balkans in eastern Europe. By the 1850s the empire was in decline and starting to **break-up**. Russia and Austria both wanted to take territory from the Ottomans.

sphere of influence
A group of countries that are controlled or influenced by another, more powerful country

> ■ Make notes on this section, using these questions to guide you:
> - How important to Austria was the relationship between Austria and Russia?
> - Why was their relationship coming under strain in the early 1850s?
> - Why did Austria hesitate in entering the Crimean War?
> - What was the impact of the Crimean War on Austria's relationship with Russia?
> - How did Russia contribute to Austria losing her grip on Italy?
>
> You should be able to explain more of the links between the factors, and you might also want to edit or improve any of the explanations that you have already noted down.

The rise of Prussia

As we know, in 1815 the Italian states had been 'restored', which meant that many of the pre-Napoleonic states were re-created and much of Italy was given over to Austrian domination so that the peninsula could not be controlled by France. Similarly, Germany was also 'restored' and a German 'confederation' was created. This was a loose political system headed by Austria, but which also gave a great deal of influence to Prussia and lots of independence to each of the individual states. This German Confederation was created so that Austria and Prussia could both have influence over the other German states but without either side dominating. It was hoped that conflict between them would therefore be lessened.

This system was not perfect however, and from the 1830s increasing rivalry between Prussia and Austria put it under strain. Austria needed Germany to remain as separate states, so that she could continue to rely on their support in maintaining her power in Europe. She also needed to co-operate with Prussia to be able to do this. However, Prussia's economic, military and political power increased greatly after 1815, and eventually Prussia sought to dominate Germany herself, and do this by uniting the German states in one political unit.

One way that Prussia sought to lessen Austria's power was to isolate her economy from the other German states, so that she could not trade with them unless she paid high **tariffs** on the exports she made to Germany. In 1834 Prussia and other important German states formed the 'Zollverein' – a customs union, which abolished import and export taxes between the member states, made each state use the same weights and measures, and which standardised customs for trade across the border to those states outside the Zollverein. Austria was not permitted to join. The Prussians argued that the non-German areas of Austria–Hungary would have made her too economically powerful for the other German states to compete with her. Austria put forward her own proposals for a customs union with the German states, but Prussia's Zollverein won out, and by 1860 Prussia economically dominated Germany, and was signing free trade agreements with Britain and France leaving Austria further out in the cold.

Prussia also looked to take advantage of Austria's weakness after she lost her traditional ally, Russia, over the Crimean War in 1854. In 1859,

tariffs
Taxes payed on goods imported into a state. Tariffs protected producers from foreign competition.

■ Make notes on this section, using these questions to guide you:

- Why were British people interested in Italy?
- What stopped Britain from taking practical steps to encourage Italian unification before the 1850s?
- What role did Britain take in encouraging unification after 1855?

You should now be able to explain even more links between this factor and some of the others. Note down any explanation of these links that you can, and review the others you have already made.

■ Concluding your enquiry

1 Look at your diagram and review your explanation for the links. Revise any that you now want to explain differently or in more detail.

2 Does the pattern of links suggest that one of the factors is more important than the others? (For example, was one factor a catalyst or cause of some of the others?) Alternatively, did two or three key factors work together to cause Italy to fall from Austria's grasp?

3 Write one or two summary paragraphs that answer the question and which explain as many links between the factors as possible.

To help organise your links, you could use concept mapping software found on the internet. Concept mapping is not mind mapping – the important thing in a concept map is the link between factors, not the factor itself.

Summary: Why did Austria lose her grip on Italy by 1860?

When [German Unity] was achieved it owed much to the window of opportunity that existed in the European power [balance] after the Crimean War.

The historian Edgar Feuchtwanger is here writing about German unification but he could just as well be describing the unification of Italy. The Crimean War did create new relationships, alliances and enemies in Europe. This new landscape allowed those Italians who were pressing for change, whether that be aggrandised Piedmont (in the case of Cavour) or a unified Italy (in the case of Garibaldi) to resist Austria's domination and bring those changes to Italy.

However, we could dig deeper and say that there were other causes. The break-up of the Ottoman Empire would probably have continued even if war had been avoided over the Crimea in 1856. This break-up would, very probably, have led to conflict between Austria and Russia. We might also say that the 1815 settlement which sought to contain France would have come under pressure sooner or later, especially after Napoleon III became President and then Emperor of France. Similarly, Prussia's economic and military power was growing independently of Austria and Russia's rivalry. We could convincingly argue that Austria would have faced a challenge from Prussia at some point. All these probable developments would have affected Austria's ability to hold on to Italy.

Interestingly, some historians now see these developments as a miscalculation for Britain and Russia, as well as more obviously for France. In supporting the destruction of Austria's power over Italy and central Europe, Britain, France and Russia allowed Prussia to rise in Austria's place. As early as 1866 British diplomats were worried that the lack of Austrian power might balance that of a rising Prussia. With Prussia winning the battle for power over Germany, and having been pushed out of Italy, Austria therefore looked eastwards in the Balkans for new territory and influence. This brought her into further conflict with Russia who, as we have seen had cultural, ethnic and religious ties with the Slavic people living there. This conflict rumbled away until 1914 when it ignited a European war which we know as the First World War. This saw the collapse of the Austrian, Russian and German Empires, great damage to the economies of Britain and France, the rise of America as a world power, a communist revolution in Russia, and the deaths of more than 30 million people, soldiers and civilians, around the world.

Garibaldi and Cavour

Giuseppe Garibaldi, 1807–82

Garibaldi was born in Nice in 1807. According to the historian G. M. Trevelyan's romantic view of Garibaldi's childhood, he was a sensitive reader of poetry but also a robust young adventurer, often playing truant from school to go swimming in the sea or hunting in the hills around the city. In 1822 he left school and worked his way up from cabin boy to captain on merchant ships. On his voyages around the Mediterranean and the Black Sea he met many revolutionary exiles from France and Italy. Garibaldi became convinced of the cause of Italian unity and in 1832 he travelled to Marseilles, met Mazzini and joined Young Italy. In 1834 he took part in a failed revolution in Piedmont and fled into exile.

Garibaldi travelled to South America in 1836 where he set up a business trading goods up and down the coast from Rio de Janeiro. Perhaps this peaceful life bored him, because by December he was fighting for the revolutionary Republic of Rio Grande do Sul against the Empire of Brazil. During this conflict Garibaldi learned how to fight a guerrilla war – using smaller bands of volunteer soldiers to fight effectively against much larger and better equipped forces. When civil war struck neighbouring Uruguay in 1842 Garibaldi commanded a legion of Italian exiles there. These volunteers wore the 'red shirts' of Argentine gauchos, and this uniform became the symbol of those who later fought with Garibaldi in Italy.

Garibaldi returned to Italy with his Brazilian wife Anita in 1848 when he heard of the revolts across the peninsula. When Piedmont's forces were beaten at Custoza on 25 July 1848 he carried on fighting the Austrians in the Alps, using the guerrilla tactics he had learned in South America, until he was pushed back into Switzerland. There followed an attempted voyage to Sicily, an invitation from the Duke of Tuscany to lead his forces, and in early November, a stand-off with Papal forces in the Romagna. News reached Garibaldi here of the revolution in Rome. More volunteers flocked to join him, and he marched to the city in early December 1848 at the head of 500 men. Garibaldi's defence of the Roman Republic, though it ended in defeat, made his reputation as a brave military leader who inspired great loyalty and in part explained why so many young men volunteered to serve with him in 1860.

△ A portrait of Garibaldi painted by the Italian artist Enrico Cadolini. The painting shows the uniform that Garibaldi's volunteers wore – in fact, they were known as the 'red shirts'.

Count Camillo Benso di Cavour, 1810–61

Cavour had a very different, much more privileged life to that of Garibaldi. Cavour's father was an aristocrat who had been able to work with, and profit from, both the Napoleonic regime before 1814 and the restored Piedmontese monarchy. Cavour spoke French and the Piedmontese dialect, and though he also learned some Italian, he was most comfortable talking in French. Despite a bright, intelligent and cheerful character, Cavour has also been described as a spoilt child. As an adult he was famous for his bad temper.

After a brief and very unsuccessful time as a page in the household of Prince Charles Albert at the age of 14, Cavour's father sent him to a military academy and then to the army, which did not suit him any more than life at court. He was too liberal for his fellow officers and did not enjoy their company. Cavour spent his time in the army reading and learning more about the liberal ideas that would inform his policies in the 1850s. He found a passion for mathematics and economics. In his mid-twenties Cavour left the army and travelled to France and Britain where he learned about agricultural and industrial development as well as Britain's parliamentary political system. Britain's wealth, power and personal liberty impressed him.

Cavour returned home in 1835 to run his family's farms, which he set about improving with energy and skill. After a scandal later in the decade when he lost a great deal of his own and friends' money on the French stock-exchange, Cavour focused more on encouraging reforms in Piedmont, founding schools, launching an Agricultural Association to improve farming and taking up journalism for liberal publications in Piedmont and abroad. From 1847 he wrote for the liberal journal *Risorgimento*, which was edited by Cesare Balbo (see pages 39–40) and in 1848 he was elected as a member of the Piedmontese Parliament. By November 1852 Cavour was the Prime Minister of Piedmont, and he held this position more or less continuously until his early and unexpected death in 1861, shortly after the Kingdom of Italy was created.

▷ This statue is part of the Cavour monument built in 1864 by Italian sculptors Ercole Villa and Giuseppe Argenti in the Piedmontese city of Vercelli. Cavour is often given this kind of pose in monuments. He is shown as a statesman, in debate or presenting an argument.

7 Was Cavour's diplomacy the main reason why Piedmont became Italy's leading state by 1860?

Reminder – As you'll know from Chapter 5, the Kingdom of Italy was only a few months old when Victor Emmanuel declared the creation of the Kingdom in March 1861. This declaration followed the Second War of Independence of 1859, in which Piedmont annexed Lombardy, Parma, Modena and much of the Papal States and, in 1860, Garibaldi's invasion of Sicily and conquest of Naples before he handed these conquests to Victor Emmanuel.

Count Cavour, Italy's first Prime Minister, died on 6 June 1861 aged 50, probably from malaria picked up while overseeing his own rice farms. His premature death caused great concern across Europe. In London *The Economist* reported how stocks and shares had been affected by the news. *The Times* of 7 June ran a long obituary praising Cavour's legacy. We have adapted parts of that obituary to show some of the main points *The Times* made about his impact on Italy.

> The biography of Cavour is the biography of [Piedmont,] the leading State of the Italian nation. [...] It became evident that all her internal reforms were but means to an end, and that this end was the consolidation of Italian liberty. He saw his opportunity and turned [the Crimean War] to Italy's advantage. He accepted, perhaps even suggested, the invitation of England to join the alliance against Russia. The alliance between Piedmont and France was Cavour's handiwork. After resigning over the Villafranca agreement, the Italian people called him back to lead Italy. Garibaldi has lived to see that Cavour and himself were following the same object by different routes.

◁ This stamp, issued in 1959 to commemorate the 1859 Second War of Independence, presents the four heroes of the *Risorgimento*. History is often presented to fit neat and exciting stories of good and evil, and the stamp shows us how Victor Emmanuel, Garibaldi, Cavour and Mazzini's stories were used to create such a 'story'. Notice that they are all facing the same direction, their images creating an appearance of unity. *The Times* obituary seems to agree with this version of events – that the great men of the *Risorgimento* were working together.

Obituaries are interesting pieces of evidence for historians. They are usually written shortly after somcone's death, as this one was, and so tend to be generous to the person they are describing. Often they have a narrative structure, telling the life of a person as a story, with a plot and a direction. In the view of *The Times* obituary, Italy was created as a direct result of Cavour's clever diplomacy and Cavour had always had a clear aim – the unification of Italy – an aim shared by Garibaldi. However, is this interpretation accurate? Was Cavour's diplomacy, over the Crimea and at Plombières, the main reason why Piedmont took the leading role in Italy?

■ **Enquiry Focus:** Was Cavour's diplomacy the main reason that Piedmont became Italy's leading state by 1860?

Four developments played a part in Piedmont becoming Italy's leading state. These were:

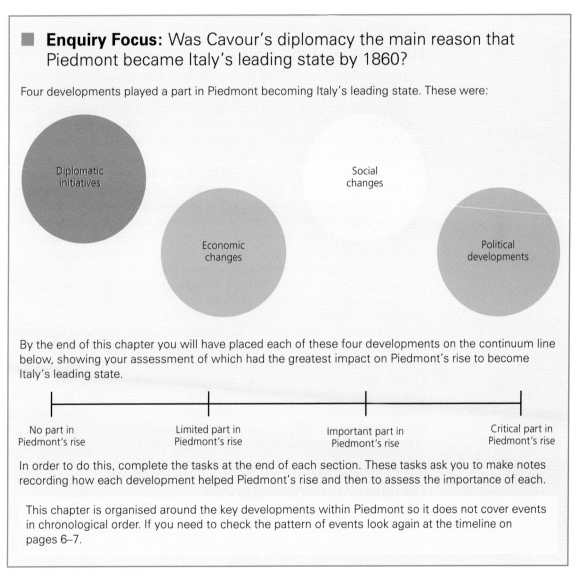

By the end of this chapter you will have placed each of these four developments on the continuum line below, showing your assessment of which had the greatest impact on Piedmont's rise to become Italy's leading state.

| No part in | Limited part in | Important part in | Critical part in |
| Piedmont's rise | Piedmont's rise | Piedmont's rise | Piedmont's rise |

In order to do this, complete the tasks at the end of each section. These tasks ask you to make notes recording how each development helped Piedmont's rise and then to assess the importance of each.

This chapter is organised around the key developments within Piedmont so it does not cover events in chronological order. If you need to check the pattern of events look again at the timeline on pages 6–7.

Political developments

The main political developments that contributed to Piedmont's changing status were:

- the impact of the *Statuto*
- the *connubio* and Cavour's control of parliamentary government
- the National Society.

Together these developments created the belief that Piedmont was providing moral leadership for the states of Italy, charting the way to a more modern society and a unified Italy.

The impact of the *Statuto*

Piedmont began the 1850s as the only state in Italy to have any kind of constitutional government. In theory the 'law of the monarchy', as the *Statuto* described itself, was a set of laws that the king and parliament had to abide by. As a result, Piedmont could claim moral leadership in Italy, as the *Statuto* guaranteed some rights and freedoms, such as the right to vote in elections to the Piedmontese Parliament (if you were rich enough), the right to free speech and to publish political opinions and rules that meant that the courts could not order anybody to be arrested without evidence. In contrast, elsewhere in Italy the rulers restored by Austria and France turned to more repressive ways of strengthening their rule: imprisoning revolutionaries, seizing money and property owned by their families, and re-imposing censorship of the press. During the 1850s the relative freedom enjoyed by the Piedmontese made it a haven for radicals and progressive liberals who wished to see change in Italy. Perhaps thousands of these people came to live in Piedmont, and turned it into a centre of information, debate and support for the idea of a unified Italy.

Ironically the *Statuto* had not been designed to restrict the powers of the king or his ministers to any great extent, or to introduce real democracy or revolutionise how the state was run. It had been granted by Charles Albert against his wishes, as a response to the threat of revolution early in 1848. When Victor Emmanuel II became king in 1849 he wanted to abolish the *Statuto* but Austria insisted that he keep it, to prevent further revolution in Piedmont. By doing this Austria contributed to Piedmont's reputation as the 'leading state'.

The *connubio* and Cavour's control of parliamentary government

Cavour cannot take credit for the granting of the *Statuto* as this was done before his rise to power. He was also not involved in the decision to retain this 'constitution' after the defeat of 1849. However, Cavour can take credit for helping the constitution to work and for helping Piedmont to develop the traditions and conventions of parliamentary politics. The survival of these political features made Piedmont more attractive to liberals and democrats from around Italy. Being the only state in Italy with a parliament also brought sympathy for Piedmont from Britain. Cavour's

◁ This lithograph of Cavour was drawn around 1860 for a book written by one of Cavour's allies, Giuseppe La Farina. It presents Cavour as a wise statesman, and this is certainly how he is often remembered in Italian national history.

skilful control of parliament also increased his reputation in Italy and abroad as an able and effective politician.

Cavour was an energetic and effective minister and by 1852 was convinced that he, and not d'Azeglio should be the Prime Minister. Cavour used the *Statuto* and the **Chamber of Deputies** expertly, alongside his knowledge of the workings and history of the British Parliament, to help him become Prime Minister and, once in power, to control the Chamber of Deputies in the Piedmontese Parliament. He recognised that many of the deputies on the left were moderates who he could work with, and that if he joined forces with them he could count on the support of the deputies on the centre left and those on the centre right. To secure this arrangement he worked with Urbano Rattazzi, the leader of the moderate left wing deputies, and helped him to get the job of Speaker of the Chamber of Deputies. This arrangement was called the *connubio* or marriage and was announced in February 1852. The *connubio* gave Cavour control of a large majority of deputies and provided a springboard that enabled him to become Prime Minister.

Once in power, Cavour kept tight control of the Chamber of Deputies, allowing him to use Parliament to support his programme of reforms and foreign policy. This control also prevented serious conflict between Parliament, the government of Piedmont and the monarch. If such a conflict had arisen, then there was a serious risk that the King might have suspended Parliament or revoked the constitution, damaging Piedmont's reputation for liberalism and for stability and reducing her claim to provide moral leadership within Italy.

Chamber of Deputies
This was the Piedmontese Parliament's lower house, like Britain's House of Commons

As an example of Cavour's control, he was able to use Parliament as a rubber-stamp to approve matters that had already been decided, or even that had already been carried out. This happened over the cost of building fortifications (in 1851 and 1857) and also over significant issues such as getting the approval of Parliament for the 1860 treaty which transferred Nice and Savoy to France. Cavour also kept control over discussions in Parliament by keeping important ministries in his own hands. At times he was not only Prime Minister but also in charge of foreign affairs, financial affairs and also held the position of Minister of the Interior.

At other times Cavour simply ignored Parliament, often in order to stop the King dissolving Parliament or declaring an end to the *Statuto*. In 1855, Parliament and the Piedmontese cabinet had both voted against Piedmont joining the Crimean War, yet Cavour was forced to declare that Piedmont would be joining the war on the side of Austria, France and Britain, because King Victor Emmanuel had already committed Piedmont to this action. In fact, the King had hinted to the French that he could use the Crimean War as an excuse to sack Cavour and threaten the *Statuto*. When Cavour found out, according to the historian Denis Mack Smith in his political biography of Cavour, the Prime Minister 'brilliantly retrieved the situation by disregarding his cabinet and suddenly deciding for war'. This policy of keeping Parliament's attention away from foreign policy and out of conflict with the King, continued with regard to the Congress of Paris of 1856 – Cavour even refused to consult his cabinet over Piedmont's position at the conference.

Piedmontese political parties

Piedmont did not have a strong political party system in the 1850s. Many viewed the idea of parties as dangerous and a sign of division and discord. Cavour believed in a 'centrist' policy; a middle way between the conservative traditionalists of the right and the liberals of the left. Moderate democrats in a Piedmontese context were those that believed in a limited amount of public involvement in politics, but still had many traditional beliefs about running a state.

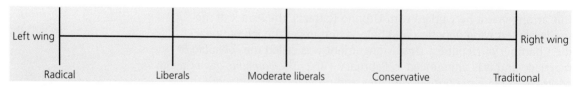

△ This diagram shows the variety of political beliefs held by deputies in the Piedmontese Chamber of Deputies. Traditionalist deputies tended to want to return to a time of autocratic rule by the King and for the Catholic Church to have an important role in welfare and education. Liberals hoped that constitutional monarchy, where wealthy Piedmontese could vote in parliamentary elections, would bring stability and progress. Radical democrats hoped to see the vote given to poor Piedmontese, and possibly for Piedmont to become a republic.

The National Society

The National Society, founded in Turin in 1857, was another political reason why middle-class liberals across northern Italy started to look to Piedmont for leadership. In her book *The Italian Risorgimento*, the historian Lucy Riall claims that 'the society played a vital role in giving the nationalist cause a base among the educated middle class'. The society emerged from meetings and correspondence in the previous two years between Daniel Manin, Giorgio Pallavicino and Giuseppe La Farina. All three had been radical Mazzinians:

- Giorgio Pallavicino, a veteran of all the revolts of 1820–21, 1831, and 1848–49, was an aristocrat whose money fuelled the organisation and paid for the publication of its journal – the *Piccolo Corriere d'Italia* which can mean the 'carrier' or the 'messenger' of Italy.

- Giuseppe La Farina, a passionate nationalist, writer and minister, who worked closely with Cavour through the 1850s. He was the secretary of the National Society.

- Daniele Manin, in 1848 sparked revolution in Venetia and led the rebels in the Venetian Republic. He was President of the National Society and his fame as the hero of Venice brought in a large number of former revolutionary supporters.

The society's members were often ex-Mazzinian radicals, who had grown disheartened at the lack of revolutionary spirit in most Italians, and were willing to support Victor Emmanuel's Piedmont, if it made any attempt to remove the Austrians and unite Italy. The success of the National Society in recruiting former radicals to the cause of Piedmontese leadership can be seen in Garibaldi's decision to join soon after it was formed, but also in the connection it formed between radicals like Pallavicino and moderates like Cavour.

The leaders of the Society met Cavour several times in the late 1850s, and were suspicious of his intentions, suspecting that he was more interested in Piedmontese aggrandisement than in Italian unity. Nonetheless, as France and Piedmont continued to develop an alliance which offered a way of expelling the Austrians from Italy, the National Society increasingly placed its support and hopes in Piedmont's leadership. In 1859 Garibaldi, by then the President of the National Society, met Victor Emmanuel. The two of them seemed to get on well, and Garibaldi's exploits over the next few years (see Chapter 8) were carried out in the name of Italy and King Victor Emmanuel, and were, in part, funded by the National Society. Therefore, the National Society played a crucial role in allowing radical and moderate Italian nationalists to work together in some cases.

The main activity of the National Society, until the Second War of Independence in 1859, was propaganda. The society printed pamphlets and newspapers, organised committees in other northern Italian states and raised money. In 1859 it took on a more revolutionary role, starting or manipulating revolts and protests in the Central Duchies and Romagna, and organising the plebiscites that formalised their annexation after the **Treaty of Turin** in 1860.

The **Treaty of Turin** was the treaty of 1860 between France and Piedmont, which gave France Nice and Savoy in return for her recognition that Piedmont had annexed Tuscany, the Romagna, Parma and Modena. See page 93.

Diplomatic initiatives

Chapters 5 and 6 have introduced some of the major diplomatic developments of the 1850s. In this chapter we will explore how these developments helped Piedmont become Italy's leading state and secondly, whether Cavour deserves all the credit for these changes. The key developments discussed below are:

- Piedmont's part in the Crimean War and the Congress of Paris 1856
- the Plombières meeting between Louis Napoleon and Cavour
- goading Austria into war
- the Treaty of Villafranca and the Treaty of Turin.

Piedmont's decision to enter the Crimean War

The Crimean War is often presented as an important stepping-stone in the story of Italian unification. That was certainly the opinion of *The Times* obituary (see page 104). The first popular historian of the *Risorgimento*, G.M. Trevelyan, in his book *Garibaldi and the Thousand* (1909), presented 'Cavour's Crimean policy' as a plan to create an alliance with France or Britain which would weaken Austria's grip on Italy. However, Denis Mack Smith takes the more balanced view that Cavour was aware of the disadvantages as well as the advantages to Piedmont taking part in the Crimean War. He knew that entering the war was very unpopular with Cavour's cabinet, the Piedmontese parliament and with the Piedmontese public. Piedmont could not afford a war, as she was still heavily in debt, still paying for the reparations to Austria from the 1848 war and for the reforms and investments that Cavour's government was making in her transport and other infrastructure projects. On the other hand, Cavour hoped that if the alliance was carefully negotiated there might be territorial or other gains if Piedmont entered the war on Britain and France's side.

In fact, it was Victor Emmanuel who was most enthusiastic about Piedmont taking part in the Crimean War. This was not because he hoped it would lead to Italian unification or because it would give Piedmont new allies in Britain and France for a future war with Austria. Instead, Victor Emmanuel wanted to go to war to gain a glorious reputation as a military power for his country and recognition as a great general for himself. He wanted to lead his forces personally, and at one point offered his services to the British and French as commander-in-chief of all their forces too. They turned him down!

So, while Cavour was in careful negotiations with the French and British over territorial or other gains from Austria, Victor Emmanuel was telling the French ambassador in Turin that Piedmont would be joining the war. If that meant sacking Cavour and the whole cabinet and declaring war himself even better – as this would be the excuse he needed to get rid of Cavour, whose furious temper and rudeness towards the monarch irritated the King. Victor Emmanuel had made no secret of his dislike of parliamentary rule, and had also hinted that a war might give him a reason to suspend the constitution. But the French ambassador told a friend, who told Cavour. Cavour was therefore forced to support entry into the war or lose his job. He carried out this volte-face very well, making a stirring speech to Parliament about lifting Piedmont's reputation and proving that her military valour was as great as that of her ancestors. However, his diplomatic attempts to gain more for Piedmont out of the war had been destroyed by Victor Emmanuel's hasty promises of Piedmontese participation to the French.

The Congress of Paris, 1856

In April 1856 Cavour went to the Paris Congress that followed the Crimean War with high expectations. He hoped that Piedmont would be rewarded with territory in Italy, perhaps Parma, in return for promising to support France in the negotiations and by reminding France and Britain of the role Piedmont had played in the war. Events did not work out as Cavour hoped. Napoleon's representative argued that Piedmont should not be allowed to take part and made it clear that France would not consider giving Parma to Piedmont. It was only as a result of Britain's support that Piedmont was given a seat at the conference table. Cavour then made attempts to play the British and the French off against each other, in order to win territorial gains, but he became increasingly panicked as it looked as if the predictions he had made to his cabinet members and the King would not turn out to be accurate. It looked as if Piedmont would not gain anything tangible from the Congress.

After the main treaty was signed, the future of Italy was discussed formally at the Congress. The French and British representatives criticised the Pope and the King of Naples for the way that they ruled central and southern Italy. However, they would not agree to ask Austria to remove her troops from the Papal States (they had been there since 1849) because France also had troops in Rome. The **Earl of Clarendon**, spoke with force and sympathy about the need for reform in Italy – especially in the Papal States and in Naples where the Pope and King of Naples ruled as autocrats. Cavour seems to have misread this sympathy as criticism of Austria and as a sign that Britain would support Piedmont in a war with Austria to liberate Italy. In mid-April he travelled to London, and caused a minor diplomatic incident when he seemed to encourage the political opposition to the government to attack Clarendon's actions in Paris. This was perhaps a clumsy attempt to force **Palmerston** and Clarendon to make a much more obvious attack on Austria's influence in Italy. Though the British continued to press for Austria's withdrawal of troops, it was clear that Cavour had misunderstood their intentions, and that war with Austria would not have British support. The historian Denis Mack Smith claims that the

George Villiers, the Fourth **Earl of Clarendon** was a senior British diplomat and Foreign Secretary from 1854 until 1858.

Henry Temple, the Third Viscount **Palmerston** was the British Prime Minister between 1855 and 1858, and then from 1859 to 1865.

importance of Cavour's diplomacy over the Crimea and its aftermath was that Cavour realised that the French were much more likely allies than the British against Austrian influence in Italy. We could go further and argue that he learned this almost by accident after making serious diplomatic errors with Britain.

Plombières and the alliance with France

Cavour's diplomatic skills were vitally important in the creation of the alliance between France and Piedmont in 1858 and then the goading of Austria into war in 1859. Cavour had to react to events as they occurred, and often this improvisation was done with skill. As we learned in Chapter 6, in January 1858 Napoleon III survived an assassination attempt by an Italian nationalist, Orsini. Cavour reacted quickly to Napoleon's understandable anger and to a threat by the French to ally with Austria against Piedmont. He placated Napoleon by suppressing radical newspapers and arresting many of those suspected of being involved in radical plots. Cavour's actions may have convinced the Emperor that France now had sufficient influence or control over Piedmont to attempt a more purposeful alliance.

Napoleon invited Cavour to Plombières to a meeting so secret that neither the French foreign minister nor the Piedmontese cabinet were informed. At this meeting the plan for war with Austria was hatched. The agreement, reported by Cavour in a letter to Victor Emmanuel, is clear about what Piedmont would get – the annexation of Parma, Modena, Lombardy and Venetia, and that a Kingdom of Central Italy would be created, made up of Tuscany and most of the Papal States. However, the letter was not clear who would rule this new Kingdom of Central Italy, or the Kingdom of Naples. This was left undecided, but Napoleon had hopes of replacing the King of Naples with one of his relatives or an ally. What also wasn't clear was that Cavour had agreed to give Savoy and Nice to France. This would have serious, if unexpected consequences.

The Times obituary that opened this chapter suggested that Cavour had the aim of unifying Italy and that his diplomacy was directed at this. The Plombières agreements and some of the letters back and forth between France and Piedmont that followed it, suggest that this was not the case. It seems that Cavour took the chance to take Tuscany and parts of the Papal States when this opportunity arose but had unification with the south of Italy forced upon him by the extraordinary actions of Garibaldi. Indeed, as late as November 1858 Cavour wrote to the Piedmontese ambassador in Paris suggesting that those living in Tuscany and in the Romagna on the other side of the Apennines were two different races that could 'never possibly be welded together'.

Goading Austria into war

Having gained an alliance against Austria, the next step was to goad Austria into a war. This was, as Christopher Duggan puts it, a 'juggling act', as Cavour needed to provoke a war so that Austria seemed like the aggressive power. If Piedmont or France was seen as the aggressor then Prussia or even Britain might intervene on Austria's behalf. In the event, Cavour's diplomacy was perhaps clumsy in this task, and he could not contain the enthusiasm of Victor Emmanuel for war, the King excitedly letting slip their plans on several occasions. Piedmont also began to spend large sums of money on building up their army. Victor Emmanuel made provocative speeches to the Piedmontese Parliament and members of the National Society tried to start revolts in Parma and Modena. It became obvious to Britain and Prussia that France and Piedmont wanted a war with Austria.

Cavour and Napoleon hoped that there would be popular revolts in northern Italy so when Austria intervened this would give Piedmont an excuse to 'defend' Italy against her. The problem was that no uprising came. By March, Prussia was threatening to support Austria if there was a war, and Russia was suggesting an international congress to discuss the situation in Italy. Cavour rushed to Paris to try to maintain Napoleon's enthusiasm for war, but the Emperor had already decided that the game was up, as by this time Britain was also putting pressure on the French not to go to war. It looked as if Cavour's diplomacy had failed and he reluctantly agreed to disarm.

What saved the plan and ignited the war of 1859 was Austria's pride. She saw that Piedmont was now isolated and therefore decided to teach the Piedmontese a lesson. Austria issued an 'ultimatum' on 23 April 1859, to de-mobilise within three days or face war. This immediately made Austria seem like the aggressor, just as Cavour and Napoleon wanted. Within three days Austria was at war with Piedmont with France as her ally.

---

1 Make detailed notes explaining:
   a) how each of these diplomatic initiatives helped Piedmont become the leading state in Italy
   b) to what extent Cavour was responsible for these initiatives.

2 Using your notes, decide where to place 'Diplomatic initiatives' on your continuum diagram and briefly note down the major reasons for your decision.

Economic changes

By 1858, Piedmont's economy and her economic links with other states in Europe, had been reformed by an energetic and ambitious Cavour. These reforms made Piedmont an attractive place for investment, an example to liberals and reformers across the peninsula, and gave her the money she needed when the war of 1859 started. During the 1850s Cavour used his interest in finance and his experiences of travelling to London and Paris, to inform his plans for Piedmont's economy. The main economic developments that contributed to Piedmont's changing status were:

■ free-trade agreements with important European countries

■ investment in **infrastructure**, especially transport

■ the increase in Piedmontese tax revenues and national debt.

Cavour believed in **free trade**. He set about removing import taxes (sometimes called 'tariffs') on wheat imported into Piedmont. This had

infrastructure
This usually refers to the physical things that a country needs to make it work well, and to enable it to develop. For instance, modern infrastructure can mean roads, railways, canals and ports. It can also refer to communications equipment such as telegraph lines

free trade
This was the idea that countries should not impose taxes on goods they imported from abroad. Those who wanted 'free trade' hoped that the increased competition from imported goods would not only lower prices, but would encourage businesses to improve their products so that they could compete better

the desired effect of lowering food prices in the kingdom. In turn this encouraged Piedmontese farmers to improve their farms so that they could increase their yields and lower their costs. In addition, it made Piedmont a trading partner for countries like Britain and France, as well as stimulating imports of raw materials that could be used in industrial development, such as building factories and transport links.

Cavour increased Piedmont's tax revenues by imposing new taxes and raising tax income during the 1850s from 91 to 164 million lire – a rise of 80 per cent. Other states such as Lombardy, only managed around 12 per cent increases and Naples saw its tax income fall by nearly 10 per cent. Some of this money paid for transport improvements. Piedmont's railway network expanded quickly during the 1850s and by 1859, Piedmont had over 850 kilometres of railway, almost as much as the rest of Italy together. Roads and canals also saw important investment. All these changes made Piedmont 'economically the most modern state in Italy', according to Stuart Woolf, in his book *A history of Italy* (1979). Piedmont was an example of economic leadership for moderates in the other Italian states, who urged their rulers to make similar changes. They also contrasted with the lack of development in Venetia and Lombardy, where the nearly bankrupt Austrian empire had to cut back on its investment in transport, and which increasingly could not find a market for the goods manufactured in its Italian provinces.

However, even the large increases in tax revenues could not pay for all Piedmont's investment. Furthermore, Cavour had to find money to make interest payments on the **national debt**, to build up Piedmont's armed forces and defences, as well as provide a secret fund for the activities of his agents and the National Society around Italy. Piedmont also had to make **indemnity payments** to Austria under the treaty that was signed after the defeat of 1849. To make all these payments, Piedmont had to borrow money from international banks. Cavour borrowed this money from the Rothschild family of bankers in Paris and others, hoping that competition between these banks would lead to lower rates of interest for Piedmont. When Piedmont could not raise more money in this way, Cavour sold government bonds to the Piedmontese people themselves and was successful, raising 35 million lire.

These changes brought economic improvement to Piedmont and led to the development of Piedmont's trading links with other countries. By the end of the decade Piedmont was producing more food, buying more imports and making more manufactured goods than any other region in Italy. She had also made important trading treaties with Britain, France and even with her traditional enemy, Austria. Private investors from France and especially Britain were also investing in Piedmontese industries. Reformers and liberals across the peninsula pointed to Piedmont as an example that their states should follow. Cavour's reforms to the way that Piedmont raised money by taxation and through borrowing allowed her to increase spending on the military as well as pay for some of the infrastructure improvements that had taken place.

national debt
The money that countries borrow to fund development, or pay their running costs. They usually do this by issuing 'bonds' – promises to pay back money with a certain rate of interest. The amount of Piedmont's national debt rose dramatically during the 1850s, from 120 million lire just before the 1848 revolutions, to 725 million lire by 1859

indemnity payment
An indemnity was often paid by countries defeated in war. These payments were part of the peace settlements and were supposed to compensate for the damage that was inflicted on the victorious country. Piedmont had promised to pay a large indemnity to Austria following their defeat in the 1848 and 1849 'First War of Independence'

> **1** Make detailed notes explaining:
>   a) how these economic developments helped Piedmont become the leading state in Italy
>   b) to what extent Cavour was responsible for these developments and initiatives.
> **2** Using your notes, decide where to place 'Economic changes' on your continuum diagram and briefly note down the major reasons for your decision.

Social changes

The main social developments that contributed to Piedmont's changing status were:

- an influx of moderate and radical migrants from other parts of Italy
- changes to the powers of the Church
- changes in education.

However, it is likely that these changes affected Piedmont's reputation more than they affected the way that people in the state actually lived.

One social development which affected Piedmont's status was the influx of 'exiles' from the rest of Italy. These were radicals and liberals who had fled from Lombardy, Venetia and other states after the failure of the 1848 revolts. Piedmont's *Statuto* and her relaxed rules on press freedoms made Turin a haven for those who wanted to discuss the possibility of Italian independence from Austria, or how the Italian states might work or trade together. Some historians estimate that tens of thousands of such exiles came to live in Piedmont. Stuart Woolf claims that 'increasingly, Turin became the centre of Italian Patriotism' and the historian Lucy Riall also describes a rapid and visible development of a 'public opinion' in this decade, which was driven by these freedoms of expression given in the *Statuto* and the influx of these political migrants. Cavour was able to take advantage of Piedmont's rising population of exiled Italian enthusiasts. He made a great display of outrage when the Lombard exiles in Piedmont found that their property in Lombardy had been confiscated by the Austrian state. Of those exiles elected to the Piedmontese Parliament some, such as Giorgio Pallavicino, were strong supporters of Cavour.

Cavour also supported the Siccardi laws, while he was a minister in d'Azeglio's government. These laws restricted the legal rights of priests and abolished separate courts for members of the Catholic clergy. They were in contrast to what was happening elsewhere in Italy, where the Church's influence was being used by other rulers to bolster their regimes. In 1855 Cavour's government passed more legislation that dissolved many monasteries and other religious houses in Piedmont. These reforms, which reduced the influence of the Catholic Church did bolster Piedmont's status as a liberal state, at home and abroad. The reforms' passage through the Piedmontese parliament was widely reported in the British press, and on a trip to England in December 1855, Victor Emmanuel was greeted by a delegation from the British protestant Young Man's Christian Association who urged him to be a 'bold and uncompromising defender of civil and religious liberty', according to a report in *The Spectator* magazine from December 1855.

For the sake of completeness, we mention here a final piece of anti-clerical legislation, the 1859 Casati Laws. These laws took control of education out of the hands of the Church, and gave it to the Piedmontese state. The Casati system would be very important in the years after 1861, when it was extended to the whole peninsula. However, as there was little time for it to take effect before the outbreak of the 1859 war, it cannot be claimed that this was an important change that Cavour made to Piedmont's standing in Italy before 1860.

---

1 Make detailed notes explaining;
  a) how each of these social changes helped Piedmont become the leading state in Italy
  b) how much Cavour can take the credit for these changes.
2 Using your notes, decide where to place 'Social changes' on your continuum diagram and briefly note down the major reasons for your decision.

Concluding your enquiry

Piedmont did gain from Cavour's diplomacy, though we should be careful not to see this as being part of a grand plan for unification. Cavour did hope to remove the Austrians from Italy and for an enlarged Piedmont to replace them as the dominant power, but his plan was vague at times, and often he had to improvise. Indeed one of his strengths was the skill of taking opportunities that arose. Cavour was able to get Italy discussed at the Congress of Paris, and skilfully negotiated with Napoleon at Plombières. There were other times when luck helped his diplomacy to succeed – the most obvious being the Austrian ultimatum in 1859 which came just as it seemed that Cavour had failed to provoke them into war. At other times his efforts seemed clumsy, for instance when he irritated the British with ham-fisted attempts to use the opposition in Britain to put pressure on Palmerston and Clarendon in 1856.

We might also argue that it was Cavour's great skill as a politician and as an economic reformer that gave Piedmont a leading status in the years before 1859. The reforms made at the cost of the Catholic Church, the relative freedom of speech, being the only state with any form of constitution and Piedmont's (relative) military strength made it the one state in Italy where liberals and radicals might both place their allegiance. Piedmont's economic reforms helped attract investment from British and French businesses, and gave Piedmont the financial resources (whether earned or borrowed) to pay for the *Risorgimento*.

■ Concluding your enquiry

1 Review the placement of the four developments on your continuum line and reach a final decision on where each should go.

2 What do you see now as being the most important factor in Piedmont's rise to Italy's 'leading state'? What are the main reasons for your choice?

3 How much credit should we give to Cavour in making these developments? Is Cavour crucial to the factor that you think was the most important? Sometimes it helps to formulate your argument by imagining what a 'devil's advocate' might argue against you. Here are two that suggest that Cavour was not responsible for the important changes that took place:

> In 1859 it was Napoleon III's ambition for France to replace Austria as the dominant power in Italy which gave Cavour the alliance he had clumsily sought from Britain at the Congress of Paris in 1856.

> The political changes which gave Piedmont the reputation as a leading state were all in place before Cavour became Prime Minster in 1852.

What evidence or points could you use to argue against these statements? Can you devise some 'devil's advocate' statements of your own?

The *Risorgimento* and history

On pages 9 and 10 we looked at the role that history sometimes plays in nation building. Now that we're approaching the end of the book we would like to consider how the idea of *Risorgimento* has changed since the early twentieth century and so take the story of unification up to the present day.

> Benito **Mussolini** was the dictator of Italy between 1922 and 1943. Though he was appointed as Prime Minister by the then King of Italy, he changed Italy's laws and created a dictatorship. His fascist ideology held that Italy should be re-invigorated through war and by acquiring an empire, by emphasising Italy's imperial past and through a focus on industrial development and a return to traditional family and gender roles.

Fascist history

In the 1920s, following the rise to power of **Mussolini** and the transition to a fascist dictatorship, historians continued to refer to the events of the 1850s and 1860s and the idea of *Risorgimento* as the birth of modern Italy. Fascist politicians also used Roman symbols and Italy's imperial past as part of their appeal to the Italian people, and presented their fascist dictatorship as the inheritors of the legacy of ancient Rome as well as the fulfilment of the more recent re-birth of Italy.

Stamps and other official images suggest that Mussolini wanted to link his regime with the *Risorgimento*. Indeed the fascist rulers wanted Italians to believe that they would finally fulfil the 'true' spirit of the *Risorgimento*, with a stress on national greatness. Fascists in Italy did not celebrate other 'great men' of the *Risorgimento*; instead they argued that liberal politicians like Cavour and his successors after 1860 had distorted and betrayed the *Risorgimento*. However, Garibaldi was seen as an acceptable figure of the *Risorgimento* because of his military success and his reputation as a man of action.

Explaining the failure of the 'liberal' state of 1870

After the Second World War and the defeat of fascism, the legacy of the *Risorgimento* was questioned by historians on the left wing of Italian politics, who sought to explain why the 'liberal' state created after 1861 had failed and become a fascist dictatorship. This analysis was led by Antonio Gramsci. Gramsci's analysis was influenced by Marxist theory that class struggle drives the historical process. His *Prison Notebooks*, written during his imprisonment by the fascists, described the *Risorgimento* as a 'failed revolution', because the leaders of the *Risorgimento* had failed to engage the mass of Italian peasants. Gramsci believed these leaders had failed to address the needs of the peasants and workers and wanted to supress working-class revolutionary politics. He believed that this weakened the *Risorgimento* and led later to fascism.

▷ Gramsci was imprisoned by the fascists between 1926 and 1934, when he was released on health grounds, but he died in 1937 aged 46. The notebooks he wrote in prison were published in the 1940s and 1950s and became part of the debate that sought to understand the failure of the Italian state in the 1920s.

Gramsci's analysis was not accepted by all Italian historians. Those who disputed his interpretation looked to Benedetto Croce. Croce was a leading figure in the defence of 'liberal' Italy, through his book *History of Italy from 1871–1915*, published in 1928.

Croce defended the achievements of the *Risorgimento* and gave Italy's leaders much more credit than Gramsci did. Croce argued that they had done what they could to create a progressive and liberal state in the face of many difficulties, especially Italy's economic and political backwardness and the local nature of her different cultures and languages. Croce claimed that, in spite of these hurdles, Italy's liberal leaders had made great strides in creating a successful political regime before the start of the First World War. Croce and his followers blamed the collapse of the liberal state in the 1920s on certain circumstances of those years – particularly the economic depression that followed the First World War and the fear of communism following the 1917 Russian Revolution.

Mack Smith and the politics of conflict

This focus on failure and on politics and politicians was taken up by the British historian Denis Mack Smith, who is a towering figure in the recent historiography of Italy. Mack Smith saw the roots of the failure of the *Risorgimento* in the political rivalry between the great men of the 1850s and 1860s, and the flawed regime that was imposed on Italy after 1860. Writing from the 1950s onwards, instead of portraying Cavour as the mastermind of unification, Mack Smith used the documents to suggest that Cavour had no grand plan, that he acted opportunistically only to increase the power of Piedmont and was afraid that a unified Italy would lead to radical revolution. For Mack Smith, unification therefore came about as a series of separate incidents and accidents. He saw Cavour as a **Machiavellian** figure whose legacy was damaging to a united Italy. Therefore, unification was not the fulfilment of Italy's destiny and was instead the result of conflict between the 'great men', men who had been presented as working together by earlier historians. The idea of a harmonious process of national re-birth seemed much less realistic when the messy and unattractive nature of the political rivalries involved in unification became better understood.

Machiavellian
Niccolo Machiavelli was an Italian political theorist and philosopher who wrote a short book called *The Prince*, which was published in 1513. The book was designed to advise Italian rulers on how best to run their states. Since then 'Machiavellian' has become a word which means a cynical and manipulative ruler who will betray friends and take every opportunity to increase his or her power

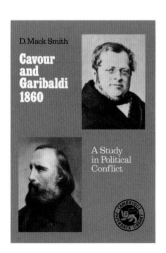

◁ Denis Mack Smith's 1954 *Cavour and Garibaldi* is subtitled 'A study in political conflict', which indicates his view that the *Risorgimento* could not be explained by the theory that Mazzini was the pen, Garibaldi the sword and Cavour the great mind which worked together to unify Italy.

New histories of Italy from the 1970s onwards

So far the focus of Italian history had been on the great men, on political movements and ideas, and on the relations between the Great Powers. Though Italian historians remained wedded to largely political readings, during the 1970s there was a new focus on economic and social history as a way of explaining the *Risorgimento* and later developments in Italian history, which came from British historians such as Stuart Woolf.

In the 1980s and 1990s political history was further side-lined as university historians were influenced by new philosophies and theories of language that became known as post-modernism. Post-modernism brought a focus on language to the study of history, and new understandings that historians constructed history and read sources in ways that were influenced by their own history, culture and experiences. From this it became clear that focusing on a single 'story' of Italian unification was unjustified. Historians realised that these events should be studied from a number of perspectives.

Historians who were influenced by these new approaches were much less likely to take a national perspective and turned their attention to local history, to the story of women or the role of different classes of people in the unification of Italy. They were much less likely to accept a story of national destiny and progress, or of *Risorgimento* and re-birth. For instance, some historians looked at the 1815 restoration states, and instead of confirming the accepted, orthodox view that such states were despotic and backward, pointed out the progressive nature of some of these states. The education system of Lombardy-Venetia for instance, was shown to be the most effective in the peninsula. These historians also placed more emphasis on the experiences of women, peasants and the middle classes. The concept of the *Risorgimento*, with its focus on the quest by people like Mazzini and Garibaldi to unify Italy, fell out of favour with historians, who preferred instead to look more at the local, social and economic circumstances of people in the restoration states to explain the political changes of the period. Historians hoped to be able to explain how unification happened, or was experienced by Italians, by focusing on local, social, economic and class issues.

Risorgimento re-born – recent histories of Italy

More recently the idea of the *Risorgimento* has had a shot in the arm. Historians like Christopher Duggan and Lucy Riall in Britain, and Alberto Banti and Paul Ginsborg in Italy, have been looking at the relationship between changes in Italian culture and the political events that led to the unification of Italy. These historians are also challenging the idea of a 'failed revolution' by explaining how ideas like romanticism, led to the rise of the idea of 'Italy' in the minds not just of a relatively small number of people, but among quite large

▷ Christopher Duggan, the academic advisor for this book, and other historians have returned to the concept of *Risorgimento* by looking at how culture, and especially the romantic movement, interacted with Italian politics.

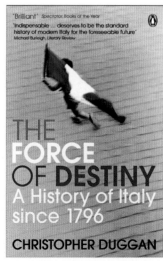

'Brilliant' *Spectator, Books of the Year*
'Indispensable ... deserves to be the standard history of modern Italy for the foreseeable future'
Michael Burleigh, *Literary Review*

THE
FORCE
OF **DESTINY**
A History of Italy
since 1796

CHRISTOPHER DUGGAN

sections of Italian society, across the peninsula and the class system. The issue of *Risorgimento* is therefore just as interesting to historians of Italy today as it was shortly after the events of unification.

So the focus on 'great men' was joined by a focus on the cultural, social and economic factors that played a role in Italy's unification. The development of Italy's historiography is, of course, part of a larger story of the way that methods and approaches have changed over time. Studies of German history, of British and other national histories are still written, but the scope and breadth of what we find interesting in the past is much wider today than it was even 30 years ago.

Popular history and official heritage

Even when academics have been arguing fiercely about the *Risorgimento*, public ideas about history have reflected other concerns and ideas. A really good example of this is the poster below. This was made in 1961, to celebrate the centenary of a united Italy, and the importance of the 'great men' of Italian unification is very clear.

The 1961 celebrations happened at a time of growing prosperity in Italy. However, the 2011 celebrations, reflected a more divided Italy, which was going through economic problems still being felt while writing this book. In 2011 the powerful and popular *Lega Nord* or 'Northern League' political party, boycotted the celebrations and instead called for the creation of a separate country made up of the prosperous north of Italy, to be called 'Padania'. For the supporters of this party, Garibaldi was a 'mercenary' who forced the south and north together, despite the obvious differences between these two halves of the peninsula.

△ A magazine cover celebrating 100 years of Italian unity.

◁ This picture from 1992 shows a Northern League politician with a poster calling for a 'second *risorgimento*', not with the aim of greater unity, but rising against the mafia and corruption that they see as coming from the south of the Italian peninsula.

8 Why was Garibaldi unable to repeat the miracle in 1862 or 1867?

In 1861 an artist painted a large picture of Garibaldi, to celebrate the incredible victories that his hero had won against the forces of the King of Naples (see pages 80 and 81). The artist, Silvestro Lega had spent part of 1848 and 1849, alongside his friends and his brother, as part of the volunteer forces fighting the Austrians in the 'first war of independence' (see Chapter 4). As you can see from the picture, below, Lega put his admiration for Garibaldi, and for the achievement in the campaign of 1860, into his painting. Garibaldi stands tall. Though he seems calm, his hand rests on his sword. This picture shows a man of action and of power, the dark clouds behind him are breaking, and perhaps the future of Italy looks brighter as they do.

By the end of this campaign Sicily then Naples had been conquered by Garibaldi and the army which started with his 'thousand' volunteers. Garibaldi's victory in 1860 is even more remarkable if we consider the long list of similar heroic expeditions that radical Italian patriots, such as **Pisacane** and the **Bandiera** brothers, undertook in the years between 1848 and 1860. All of these attempts ended in failure, and the death, exile or imprisonment of those concerned. If we also bear in mind that when Garibaldi left Piedmont in 1860 he went without any official support, and that his thousand volunteers were unarmed, then the events of 1860 seem to be even more miraculous.

In June 1857 Carlo **Pisacane** took a handful of followers and 300 escaped prisoners to start a revolt in Naples. They were attacked by peasants when they landed in Calabria, many were killed and Pisacane committed suicide.

See page 39 for information on Attilio and Emilio **Bandiera**.

▷ This painting was made in 1861, in the year following Garibaldi's campaign. It captures a popular heroic view of Garibaldi from the time – he is a thoughtful, but tall and powerful figure.

Just one year later, in 1862, newspapers around the world published this engraving of Garibaldi (right) that was very different.

In 1862, when Garibaldi had again marched thousands of volunteers from Sicily towards Rome he was attacked by Italian troops, in the region of Aspromonte in the far southern tip of the Italian peninsula. They stopped Garibaldi attempting to take Rome by force and he was shot in the ankle and arrested. As a result, these two pictures, even if we do not take them at face value, show very different attitudes towards Garibaldi. In the space of just two years Garibaldi has gone from being shown as an upright symbol of purpose and bravery, to a downcast prisoner who had failed in his quest to give Italy her capital city – Rome. In 1867 Garibaldi's final attempt to take Rome was stopped by the French who easily overpowered his last group of volunteer fighters, this time at Mentana near Rome.

△ Drawn by French artist Jean Adolphe Baunce and published by many newspapers across the world as news of Garibaldi's wounding and defeat spread, this picture presents the Italian hero as being much older, downcast and injured.

■ **Enquiry Focus:** Why was Garibaldi able to achieve a miracle in 1860, but unable to repeat the miracle in 1862 or 1867?

You have already completed causal enquiries in earlier chapters. This time we would like you to decide the best way of completing this chapter's enquiry. You will be looking for **factors**, the reasons that help us understand

a) how Garibaldi achieved his remarkable victories in 1860, when he conquered the Kingdom of the Two Sicilies and handed them to Victor Emmanuel

b) why these remarkable victories could not be repeated in 1862 and 1867 when he attempted to take Rome for the new Kingdom of Italy.

Your task is to identify and assess the relative importance of the factors. This means you do more than simply list them – you need to explain how they affected Garibaldi's victory and then his failure, and explain which of the factors were more important than others in either causing or preventing his success. So, you need to think carefully about how to record your thinking as it develops during your reading, your overall answer when you have finished and the details which support the conclusions that you draw.

A **factor** is a reason or set or reasons that enabled or caused an event to happen. Be careful! A factor is not just an event, it is a reason that this event happened.

123

Garibaldi's plans

▷ Garibaldi's 1860 expedition.

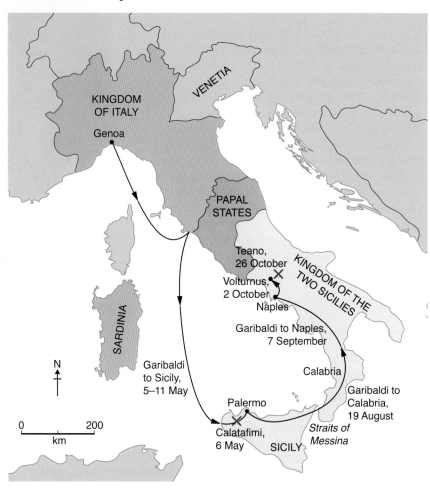

Eventually **Crispi** became part of Italy's political establishment and even became Prime Minister.

■ **Think about**

Which factors might explain why Garibaldi's expedition was a success?

Cavour's decision in 1859 to give Nice and Savoy to the French (in return for their recognition of Piedmont's annexation of Parma, Modena and Tuscany), made Garibaldi and other radicals regard Cavour as their 'bitter enemy', according to historian Denis Mack Smith. Many radicals thought that they should fight on until the whole of Italy was united. Early in 1860 Garibaldi was preparing a revolt in Nice, trying to gather supporters and arms, but his close friend Francesco **Crispi** had different ideas. Crispi was a Sicilian and a radical Italian nationalist who hoped to create a republican Italy. He persuaded Garibaldi that the best place to cause an uprising was Sicily. Sicily had been in what Duggan calls a 'febrile state', a state of rebellions, in February and March 1860. Crispi felt that if Garibaldi travelled south to Sicily, they could start a revolt that would enable them to take Sicily and possibly the mainland Kingdom of Naples itself. Garibaldi changed his plans and prepared to sail south.

Cavour's 'terrible dilemma'

Garibaldi's actions left Cavour on what the historian Christopher Duggan calls 'the horn of a terrible dilemma'. This dilemma was two-fold. Firstly, if Garibaldi's actions threatened the Pope in Rome, the Austrians or the French might intervene. This intervention might include the invasion of the new Kingdom of Italy, which therefore could be lost almost immediately after it had been created. Secondly, even if the French and Austrians didn't intervene, Garibaldi might set himself up as dictator of the south or set up a republic from where radicals could threaten the new kingdom.

However, early in 1860 Cavour's position with Victor Emmanuel and in the new Italian Parliament was so weak that he couldn't openly oppose Garibaldi's expedition. The King had already hinted that he thought the expedition was a good idea and had also told Garibaldi's supporters that he wanted to sack Cavour. In addition, it was not just the radical left-wing deputies in the Chamber of Deputies who objected to Nice and Savoy being given to France. Prominent members of the Cabinet, such as the Minister of War, General Fanti also threatened to resign. If Cavour directly opposed Garibaldi in this atmosphere he feared that he would lose his position, either by being replaced by the King, or through losing the support of a majority of deputies in the Chamber.

It seems that Cavour did what he could, behind the scenes, to ensure that the expedition was a failure. Mack Smith suggests that Cavour 'rather drifted before events' and 'that such influence as Cavour did have on events in these few days was used less to help than to deter and thwart Garibaldi.' So, while he could not actually arrest Garibaldi, or command him not to go, Cavour confiscated 12,000 guns and their ammunition from warehouses in Milan where they had been stockpiled for Garibaldi to use on expedition to Nice, where he hoped to disrupt the planned annexation by France.

> **Think about**
>
> Why was Cavour unable to stop Garibaldi from setting out for Sicily?

Garibaldi's victory in Sicily and Cavour's increasing desperation

On the night of 5 May Garibaldi's expedition set out from Genoa. On 7 May election results were announced that gave Cavour a comfortable majority in the Chamber of Deputies, and this gave him more room to act against Garibaldi. He sent an order to Admiral Persano to arrest Garibaldi's expedition en-route. Persano telegraphed back for confirmation of this order but, by the time he received a reply, Garibaldi had slipped by.

On 11 May Garibaldi landed in Sicily and five days later beat a larger and better armed Neapolitan army at the battle of Calatafimi. The victory was unexpected and dramatic, adding to Garibaldi's amazing reputation as well as the woes of the Neapolitan forces. One of Garibaldi's men wrote in his diary just before the battle that, 'there is a magic in his look and in his name. It is only Garibaldi they want.' After this victory, Garibaldi's reputation in Sicily grew and many peasants joined the fighting. By the end of May the island's capital, Palermo had fallen to the rebels.

> **Think about**
>
> What difference did Calatafimi make? What factors might help us explain Garibaldi's success in 1860?

At this point Cavour again tried to stop Garibaldi using Sicily as a base to attack Naples. He sent his trusted ally La Farina to Sicily, armed with posters which announced 'We want annexation!'. These posters were designed to convince people that there was popular support for joining Sicily to the new Kingdom of Italy. La Farina set about persuading the local aristocracy that annexation was the only way to stop radicals from over-running the island. However, before La Farina was successful in engineering annexation, Garibaldi expelled him from the island. Garibaldi wanted to retain control of Sicily. Although he claimed to rule in Victor Emmanuel's name, he planned to use Sicily as a launch pad for an invasion of Naples.

The European powers and the Straits of Messina

Britain and France were both unsure what to do about the continuing success of Garibaldi's expedition. The British Cabinet's discussions suggest they had become suspicious of both Cavour and Napoleon, following the annexation by France of Nice and Savoy, and that there was much more support for Garibaldi, even if they were alarmed that his actions in Italy might spark a war between France and Piedmont or Austria and Piedmont. They therefore decided on a policy of non-intervention in Italy.

GARIBALDI THE LIBERATOR;

Or, The Modern Perseus.

◁ This cartoon, published in the British magazine *Punch* in June 1860, shows a view from Britain of Garibaldi's expedition. There are some interesting symbols in this cartoon – Garibaldi is wearing a helmet that resembles a Phrygian cap (see page 66), Sicily is shown as a woman chained to a rock and being threatened by the sea monster 'Bomba'. Bomba was the nickname given to King Ferdinand of Naples because of his use of naval cannon in attacking the Sicilian rebels of 1848. Use the guidance on page 72 to see if you can understand the cartoonist's view of Garibaldi.

Napoleon had also announced a policy of non-intervention in Italy but he was very concerned about Garibaldi's actions in the south. Although not a supporter of the Bourbon dynasty in Naples, Napoleon feared the possibility that a powerful Italian state would be created on his borders if north and south were united. He also worried that a unification forced on the south would not work and that the traditional rivalries and differences between the regions of Italy would instead create an unstable country. Napoleon preferred the idea of a confederacy in Italy, so that these local differences could be recognised and so that the Pope's position could also be respected. French troops had been protecting the Pope since 1849 and Napoleon needed to remain as the Pope's protector, in order to head off criticism from the Catholic majority in France.

Napoleon therefore proposed that the British and the French abandon the policy of non-intervention. He also made fevered attempts to get Cavour to agree to an alliance with the Bourbons of Naples. This would oblige Cavour to act to stop any attack by Garibaldi on Naples. The King of Naples, in desperation, agreed to this. To make this arrangement more attractive to the Sicilians and to the British, the King also agreed to give the island independence, as well as announcing a constitution and parliamentary representation. Napoleon also suggested that the British and French navies work together to stop Garibaldi from crossing the Straits of Messina from Sicily to the mainland of the Kingdom of Naples. However, all his efforts were a failure. Britain flatly refused to agree to joint naval action against Garibaldi and instead re-affirmed her policy of non-intervention. With no-one to prevent him, Garibaldi crossed the Straits and on 19 August landed his troops in Calabria. The last chance for France to stop Garibaldi had been missed.

> **Think about**
>
> Why did Britain and France not act to stop Garibaldi?

Cavour attempts to regain the initiative; the fall of the Bourbon monarchy of Naples

Cavour seems to have encouraged the French to believe Piedmont would enter an alliance with the King of Naples, but it is possible that this was a ruse while he figured out the likelihood of Garibaldi's expedition being successful. As it became more likely that Garibaldi would succeed, Cavour realised that the Kingdom of the Two Sicilies was unlikely to survive. However, he was still deeply concerned that the French might intervene to protect the Pope, and worried that Garibaldi intended to hold on to the Kingdom of Naples as a dictator, threatening the new northern Kingdom of Italy. Cavour tried to seize the initiative and cause a rebellion in the city of Naples before Garibaldi reached there, so that Piedmontese troops could invade with the excuse of stopping the trouble. Admiral Persano was sent with a fleet to wait by the coast just off the city of Naples and Cavour sent agents into Naples to start revolts, so that the soldiers on board Persano's ships could then be landed in order to 'restore order'. However, the Neapolitans refused to revolt, and instead preferred to wait for Garibaldi.

Garibaldi marched from the coast, and the Bourbon army retreated ahead of him. Naples fell to Garibaldi's forces without resistance and Francis III, the last of the Bourbon kings, left in early September 1860. Garibaldi entered the city of Naples by train and was greeted by crowds of cheering supporters. The final steps took place in a series of battles with

Think about

What factors might explain Garibaldi's success on the mainland?

the Neapolitan army on the Volturno River, and by early October Garibaldi was victorious. He then headed north towards Rome and what remained of the Papal States.

Cavour's gamble

Cavour was 'forced to take one of the biggest gambles of his career', according to Christopher Duggan. Cavour warned Napoleon that the Pope was threatened. He persuaded the French Emperor to agree to Piedmont invading the Pope's territory, not only in order to stop Garibaldi, but also to prevent the formation of a radical republic. Cavour was able to use the arrival of the radical Mazzini in Naples as an illustration of this risk. The French agreed to Piedmont's intervention. Cavour sent more agents into the Papal States to start a small revolt, which was his excuse to send in the army.

The Piedmontese army marched south, as Garibaldi's army was fighting the Bourbon army at the Volturno River and making its way north. The Papal army was not easily defeated, and many peasants joined the fighting, against the Italian army. Mack Smith writes that this was effectively a civil war and that the 'fighting was conducted with [...] bitterness and cruelty on both sides'. Only Papal forces in uniform were recognised by the Italian army as legitimate enemy fighters. Peasants or priests who fought against the Piedmontese forces were executed. Mack Smith suggests that the inhabitants 'did not easily forget this kind of treatment', and this resentment caused on-going problems for the new Italian state (see Chapter 9).

The meeting at Teano

▷ This picture, published in the popular Italian news magazine *Domenica del Corriere*, shows how Garibaldi and Victor Emmanuel's meeting was presented in 1960, the centenary of the handshake which gave the south of Italy to the northern Kingdom.

Cavour's decision did stop Garibaldi from attacking the Pope. Piedmontese forces reached the border with Naples in ten days. Garibaldi now had no route to Rome, other than by attacking the forces of Victor Emmanuel, under whose name the expedition had fought. He therefore chose to hand over his conquests to the King.

Victor Emmanuel and Garibaldi met on 26 October 1860 at Teano in the Papal States. They greeted each other warmly, the King shaking Garibaldi's hand as Garibaldi effectively gave the south to him. By March 1861 the carefully organised plebiscites had brought predictably huge votes for annexation by Piedmont in Naples, Sicily and the Papal States and the Kingdom of Italy was proclaimed.

> ■ **Think about**
>
> Why did Garibaldi not force an attempt on Rome in 1860?

Garibaldi's second attempt on Rome

By 1861 Garibaldi was planning a second attempt on Rome. Cavour was now dead and without Cavour's influence, Victor Emmanuel had an even freer hand in foreign affairs. The King had been supplying Garibaldi with arms and money to raise another volunteer army. The original plan had been for Garibaldi to attack Austrian territory somewhere on the Dalmatian coast. At the same time Victor Emmanuel was sending encouragement to Hungarians rebelling against Austria. He hoped to spark another war with Austria, in which France and possibly Britain would come to Italy's aid, and which would allow Italy to claim territory such as Venetia and perhaps even Greece. Before the attack could take place however, the King got cold feet, possibly because the plan had been leaked to France and Britain, and their ambassadors had made it clear that they would not support it. Some of Garibaldi's followers were arrested on the border with Austria, but quickly released. Garibaldi himself was not arrested and Victor Emmanuel continued to boast that he had plans for Garibaldi's volunteers.

In June 1862, Garibaldi, perhaps with the approval of Victor Emmanuel, went to Sicily – it is not clear why. Denis Mack Smith suggested that Sicily was to be Garibaldi's base for an attack on Greece. A Piedmontese ship was given to Garibaldi and weapons and ammunition were stockpiled for his volunteers at Messina. However, when Garibaldi reached Sicily he decided to use his volunteers for another attempt on Rome, probably with Victor Emmanuel's secret approval. Mack Smith suggests that Victor Emmanuel hoped to repeat the tactics of 1860, hoping that the people of Rome would rise up in support of Garibaldi and then Italian forces could invade the remainder of the Papal States in the name of 'restoring order'. In Turin, Victor Emmanuel's foreign minister suggested to the Chamber of Deputies that Rome would soon be part of the Kingdom of Italy.

▷ Garibaldi's second and third attempts on Rome.

N

Florence

Rome
✕ Mentana,
3 November 1967

Naples

SARDINIA

Calabria

Palermo

✕ Aspromonte,
29 August 1862

Straits of
Messina

SICILY

0   200
   km

■ **Think about**

Why was Garibaldi's expedition weaker in 1862 than 1860?

Throughout July and August Garibaldi trained his volunteers on Sicily. According to Christopher Duggan, these were not the same type of volunteers as 'the well-educated students who had made up the backbone of the Thousand' in 1860, but poor unemployed Sicilians who joined up for the wages and because they believed this second expedition was backed by the King in Turin. Garibaldi collected weapons left in Messina and set off on 24 August across the Straits of Messina to Calabria.

When Napoleon III realised that Garibaldi intended to make an attempt on Rome, he sent a naval detachment to the Bay of Naples, signalling his disapproval and making a clear threat to intervene. At the same time the people of Rome completely failed to rise up in anticipation of their liberation by Garibaldi. It was therefore clear to Victor Emmanuel that he could not use the excuse of restoring order to justify an invasion of Rome. Instead he declared martial law in the south and sent General Cialdini and the Italian army to stop Garibaldi.

Aspromonte and Garibaldi's hesitation

The Italian army met Garibaldi's volunteers near the Aspromonte mountains on the 29 August 1862. Garibaldi had already tried to avoid a direct conflict by taking a route away from Cialdini's forces but he was caught in the woods near the town. Garibaldi ordered his troops not to fight their brother Italians, but some shots were fired from both sides. Garibaldi was shot in the ankle, a wound from which he never fully recovered, and was arrested (see the illustration on page 82). By October he was released and returned to his home on the island of Caprera.

In 1864 Victor Emmanuel recognised that they could not immediately have Rome as the capital of the new Italy. In an agreement with France, Italy promised to make Florence its capital and renounce all claims on Rome. In return France withdrew her forces from Rome. It now looked as if Italy had given up any hopes of taking Rome.

The annexation of Venice and the defeat of 1866

In 1866 there was a brief war between Prussia and Austria (see page 82). Italy took part as Prussia's ally and hoped to defeat Austria's forces and take control of the territory of Venetia and the city of Venice. However, Italy's army and navy proved to be no match for the better supplied and better trained Austrian forces. Italy was defeated on land and sea, though Garibaldi's troops did win several victories. During the peace negotiations at the end of the Austro–Prussian war, Austria did cede control of Venetia. However, in a final insult to Italy and in order to reflect the fact that Austria had not been defeated by Italian forces, Austria gave Venetia to France, who then gave it to Italy.

Victor Emmanuel's plans and Garibaldi's final attempt on Rome

Italy's reputation as a military power was therefore in tatters. To make things worse, years of civil unrest (known as 'the Brigands' War') in the south and especially in Sicily after late 1860, de-stabilised the kingdom (see page 135). Many southerners objected to rule from Piedmont as they felt that Italy had not been united but taken over by the northern kingdom.

By 1866 Victor Emmanuel was facing calls from his cabinet to reduce his spending, but the King resented Parliament interfering in his private life as well as restricting his power as monarch. It may have been the desire to regain control over politics, or simply to increase his prestige that gave Victor Emmanuel the idea of encouraging Garibaldi to make another attempt on Rome. Some of Garibaldi's allies were worried that this latest attempt was a trick – indeed, Victor Emmanuel confided to the French Ambassador that another expedition by Garibaldi would give the King the excuse to massacre Garibaldi's volunteers and rid him of this radical threat. Denis Mack Smith puts it this way: 'The King intended to enter Rome as the conqueror of both Garibaldi and the Pope'.

> ■ **Think about**
> Why did Victor Emmanuel's plans make it less likely that Garibaldi could create a second miracle in 1867?

131

Garibaldi left Caprera on 17 October 1867, but it immediately became obvious that Victor Emmanuel's plans would not work. Napoleon III, alarmed at the volunteers massing in Florence, made it clear that he would defend the Pope if he was attacked. Victor Emmanuel's government was thrown into chaos and Prime Minister Rattazzi resigned because the King had changed his mind about invading the Papal States. Victor Emmanuel cast around desperately for a new prime minister, but several candidates turned down his request, one even demanding that the King abdicate for having created such a dangerous situation.

In the meantime French forces were sent back to Rome. Despite small uprisings the people of Rome again failed to revolt in support of Italy or Garibaldi. There was a short battle at Mentana in the Papal States on 3 November 1867, which ended in defeat and another arrest for Garibaldi. French forces had not even engaged Garibaldi, who was defeated by the Papal army. Garibaldi returned to Caprera, and refused to take part in any of the King's schemes again.

■ Concluding your enquiry

1 Look again at the factors that you have noted down. For each one write a sentence that explains why they helped Garibaldi achieve his miracle, or how they prevented him from succeeding in 1862 or 1867.

2 Now you have thought carefully about the reasons for the failures in 1862 and 1867, compare them with the reasons for success in 1860. What had changed between these dates, and what was different about the circumstances of 1860 and 1862 or 1867?

3 Why was Garibaldi unable to repeat the miracle of 1860? What was the most important reason? Write a paragraph that sums up your overall argument.

Summary: Why was Garibaldi able to work a miracle in 1860, but not in 1862 and 1867?

In 1860 Sicily had already seen revolts against King Ferdinand II, building on a long history of attempted revolution and rejection of rule from Naples. Sicily was therefore an ideal place for Garibaldi to start a revolt against Naples, especially as nationalists in the south were enthusiastic about a national Kingdom of Italy following the war of 1859 and wanted to join Garibaldi's volunteer forces. At the same time Cavour was too weak at the beginning of the expedition to stop Garibaldi and, as it became more likely that Garibaldi would succeed, Cavour saw that Piedmont might even benefit.

Furthermore, Garibaldi's reputation as a military leader had followed him from the heroic defence of Rome in 1849. The victory at Calatafimi seemed a miracle that enhanced this reputation, giving his followers confidence and instilling fear into those who faced him. This explains how Garibaldi's army grew, and why Neapolitan forces seemed to melt away before him until the last stand at the Volturno.

Garibaldi was also helped by France who was unable to intervene because it had agreed with Britain not to do so, and by the collapse in Austria's power in the peninsula in the 1859 war. Napoleon may well have ordered his troops to fight Garibaldi if the expedition had threatened Rome. However, Napoleon was reluctant to annoy Britain so it was convenient for him to let Cavour order Italian troops to stop Garibaldi at the border with the Papal States, even if this meant that Victor Emmanuel was handed more Papal territory as well as Naples. There was never any question of Garibaldi fighting Victor Emmanuel's forces, which explains why the expedition ended with the handshake at Teano.

This last point is an important reason why Garibaldi was unable to repeat the miracle of 1860. At Aspromonte Garibaldi showed that he was reluctant to shed blood in fighting between Italians, as he quickly surrendered rather than attack the army of King Victor Emmanuel. The fighting in 1867 was also brief. By then Garibaldi had grown tired of his role in setting up intrigues for the King's farfetched schemes, and this, along with his advancing age (he was almost 60 in 1867 and still suffered from the wound received at Aspromonte), and the poor quality of the volunteers in 1862 and 1867 also explain his lack of appetite for battle.

Garibaldi might have had more success in Victor Emmanuel's schemes had support from the King been more concrete. In 1862 and 1867. Having set up both situations, Victor Emmanuel was unwilling to commit to an invasion of the last part of Papal territory because of the attitude of France and the risk that Italian forces would have to fight the French garrison in Rome.

This leads us to the most important reason why Garibaldi's miracles weren't repeated after 1860 – the French protection of the Pope. Napoleon's consistent attitude after 1860 was that Rome was not to become part of the Kingdom of Italy, and that France would act to protect the Pope's position. Despite Victor Emmanuel's brinkmanship it became clear that Napoleon's position was immovable – indeed, it wasn't until French troops left Rome in 1870 that Italian forces attacked and defeated Papal troops and absorbed Rome as its capital.

Was unification a glorious success?

The monument pictured here is known as the Vittoriano, as it was built to honour Victor Emmanuel, the first king of a united Italy (though he kept his Piedmontese title as Victor Emmanuel II). Its official title is the *Altar of the Fatherland* and it symbolises a united Italy. The size and ornateness of *Il Vittoriano* certainly suggest that it is celebrating a glorious achievement – the re-birth or *Risorgimento* of Italy – both in the 1880s when it was begun and by 1925 when it was completed.

However, from Garibaldi's handover of the south of Italy in October 1860 many Italians questioned whether unification would be a success. Massimo d'Azeglio, the former Piedmontese Prime Minister, wrote in 1866 that 'We have made Italy, now we must make Italians', reflecting the worry of many in the north that a new national character had to be formed. Divisions certainly existed, exemplified by the northern politician Luigi Farini who believed the south to be full of 'barbarians'. Others, like Mazzini, who wanted to see Italy reborn as a result of popular, radical revolt, feared that Italy could not really be united through Piedmont's conquest of all the other states.

Many of the events following 1860 did very little to reassure those who believed that Italian unification was not the moment of glory that had been hoped for. Economic troubles, an ongoing divide between the north and south, political instability and eventually the rise of fascism convinced many that unification was not a glorious success. This concluding chapter explores the reasons why true unification was so difficult to achieve.

autonomy
In this context autonomy means giving each area a measure of control over some aspects of government and administration, perhaps over things like taxation, education, health care and other local services

Piedmontisation, 1860–69

Despite the hope of some democrats and nationalists that the Italian states might be allowed to keep some of their different laws and customs, the conquest of the south by Garibaldi and the chaos that followed it, convinced northern politicians that too much **autonomy** would lead to the break-up of the new state.

Instead, a process known as 'Piedmontisation' saw the authorities in Piedmont impose her laws and *Statuto* across the rest of Italy. The earliest signs of this approach appeared in titles. Victor Emmanuel was still known as the II, and not Victor Emmanuel I, as he was the second king of Piedmont to have this name. The first meeting of the new Italian parliament in February 1861 was called the eighth parliament, not the first. Northern and Piedmontese officials were appointed across the peninsula and all states had Piedmont's legal code imposed on them, along with the voting system, although Christopher Duggan estimates that only one in ten men over the age of 25 owned enough property to be able to vote.

For many critics the Italian Parliament was too fond of talking, of speeches full of rhetorical flourishes and faction-fighting instead of forging national feeling through bravery and heroic actions. Furthermore, after the death of Cavour in 1861 Piedmont's prime ministers could not match his leadership and management of the different factions in Parliament.

The Piedmontese education system was also imposed across the peninsula as part of a drive to provide a 'national education' and to increase levels of literacy. In 1861 about 25 per cent of the population could read – in Britain the rate was around 60 per cent. However, many of the other states in Italy already had education systems much better than Piedmont's, especially Lombardy and Tuscany, so the imposition of the Piedmontese system was a step backwards for them. By 1870 there had been only limited success – with a literacy rate of 30 per cent, compared with 76 per cent in the UK.

△ A 10 lira coin from 1863. Notice how, despite being the first King of a united Italy, Victor Emmanuel retained the title 'II' – reflecting the legacy of his Piedmontese-Sardinian kingdom.

The Brigands' War

One of the darkest aspects of the 1860s was the brutal repression of opposition in the south. Although the government in Turin called this a war against 'brigands' it was more like a civil war. Many officers of the army of Naples joined the Italian army, on generous terms, but many ordinary soldiers and peasants took to the hills to oppose the new government. There are accounts of crucifixions, burnings and shootings, the murder of officials and the destruction of towns. Approximately 100,000 Italian soldiers were used to suppress the troubles. The unrest and rebellion continued for years afterwards.

▷ Carmine Crocco was a leader of one of the most successful brigand armies. He received support from the King of Naples in exile, and held off the new 'Italian army' until 1864 when he fled to the Papal Sates.

Unification completed

Despite continuing evidence that political unification had not yet created a sense of a single nation, the process was completed with the annexation of Venice in 1866 and of Rome in 1870.

The annexation of Venice, 1866

Venice and Rome still remained outside the new state but many hoped that they would soon become part of the new Italy and that the nation would be strengthened by defeating Austria. Tensions between Austria and Prussia had been increasing and by 1866 Prussia was ready to challenge Austria. In 1866 Italy made an alliance with Prussia agreeing that, in return for Italy fighting against Austria, she would receive Venetia. At the same time Austria signed a treaty with France to keep them out of the war against Austria, and Napoleon offered a deal with Austria to give Venetia to Italy as the price of Italian neutrality. However, Victor Emmanuel felt that Italy was honour-bound to join the war and that a military victory was an opportunity to forge Italian national pride.

Austria was defeated by Prussia but Italy performed very badly. Custoza was, yet again, the venue for defeat at Austria's hands in June 1866. The Austrians actually suffered more casualties but the Italian army lost because of poor leadership. At the naval battle of Lissa in July, Austria's smaller force defeated a much larger Italian fleet, again because of poor leadership. Only Garibaldi managed to inflict a defeat on the Austrians, at Bezzecca on 21 July. The war of 1866 was a humiliation made worse when Austria, disdainful of the defeated Italians, refused to hand over Venice directly. Instead it was given to France, and then France gave it to Italy.

The annexation of Rome, 1870

As we saw in Chapter 8, Garibaldi twice attempted in the 1860s to take control of Rome. In 1862, he was wounded by Italian troops at Aspromonte. In 1864, Minghetti, another new Prime Minister, agreed with Napoleon that French troops would leave Rome in return for Italy making Florence the new capital. They left in 1866 and, in 1867, Garibaldi tried to take Rome again with another band of volunteers. This time he was stopped by Papal troops at the Battle of Mentana. Napoleon sent French troops back to Rome and they stayed until 1870.

In 1870, war was declared between Prussia and France and, in preparation for the war, French troops were withdrawn from Rome. In September 1870, Napoleon and thousands of his troops were captured at the Battle of Sedan. Once Napoleon was captured, the way to Rome was clear and Italy acted. Victor Emmanuel II gave Pope Pius IX the option of an amicable solution to Rome's future, guaranteeing him certain rights, powers and securities if he allowed Rome to become part of the new Italy. Pius refused the offer. On 20 September 1870, after only token resistance, Italian troops broke through the walls of Rome at Porta Pia. It was not until 1929 that the Church finally gave up its claim on Rome, settling only for the recognition of the Vatican City as a separate state.

Continuing opposition from the Catholic Church

The Church had been able to use its control of education across Italy as a way of maintaining her influence on young Italians, and resented her loss of power through schools. However, the Church's objections to the new state went much further than this. In 1864 Pius IX published the Syllabus of Errors, a long list of things that the Church did not like about the way the modern world was developing generally and about the new united Italy in particular. Importantly, it also reasserted the Pope's temporal power and although the Church could not impose these ideas, the Syllabus did contribute to the way that support for a united Italy drained away in the south in the 1860s and polarised opinion across Italy.

The army

Italy's new national army consisted of the volunteer armies of Lombardy, the remains of the small militias of the Central Duchies of Tuscany, Modena and Parma, officers from Naples and the Piedmontese army. The army, it was hoped, would be a school where young men from across the peninsula would learn to be 'Italians', and which would provide glorious feats of bravery to act as an example to the rest of Italy. These hopes were not realised and the army also became a focus for resentment, caused by the Piedmontese tradition of conscription being imposed on the rest of the peninsula. Many Italians became suspicious of the army as a symbol of control from Piedmont. In addition, the government's decision that it was risky to station troops in barracks in their home regions led to troops being moved to regions they did not know. This left soldiers thrown together in barracks with men who did not share their language and they were also resented by the local people they lived among.

Political weaknesses

In 1878 Victor Emmanuel II died. His funeral was a spectacular memorial for the first King of a united Italy. Tens of thousands of people gathered in Rome to see the cortege and the symbols of unity that decorated the route. Victor Emmanuel became a symbol of unity after his death but his son, the rather dull Umberto I, was not a figure to inspire national feeling. There was already a continuing fall in the reputation of Parliament and the Italian government. Under the emerging tradition of *trasformismo*, parliament produced governments that maintained the status quo and defended the interests of the rich and powerful, rather than being a place of conflict between politicians of the left and right and making changes to benefit all Italians.

In 1882 the government, extended the right to vote to 2 million Italians, about 7 per cent of the population. With this restricted number of voters, electoral corruption remained rife and the national parliament's reputation did not rise. Despite some improvement in Italy's economic situation, from the 1880s there were increasing numbers of strikes and unrest caused by dissatisfaction with working conditions and low pay, along with an increased support for socialism.

trasformismo
This refers to the practice of governments and changing coalitions, being formed from those left and right wing deputies who seemed willing to be 'transformed' into government supporters. Politicians such as Agostino Depretis and Francesco Crispi would maintain their positions by giving ministerial positions to Deputies from the left and the right. This led to short-term policies which did not try to solve some of Italy's long-term problems. It also led to a reputation that politicians lacked conviction

War, empires, and the rise of fascism and Mussolini

In 1896 Italy attempted to form an empire, partly to create a sense of pride and unity in Italy, by invading Abyssinia in 1896. However, this culminated in five thousand Italians being killed in a humiliating defeat. Italy invaded Libya in 1911 in a second attempt to build an empire. Although this invasion was successful, it left Italy with even more debts and with the expenses of running a colony which did not bring in enough money to pay for itself. However, in Italy the first quarter of the twentieth century was overshadowed by the First World War. Five million Italians fought in terrible conditions, with low morale that was not helped by the humiliating defeat at Caporetto in October 1917. The end of the war had important political consequences for Italy. She did not gain as much territory as had been hoped from the peace negotiations, and the economy entered a severe depression as the government stopped spending large amounts of money on fighting the war.

Such rapid change and hardship led to widespread protests. 1919 and 1920 became known as the 'Red Years' or *Biennio Rosso* because of a wave of strikes led by the socialists. One of the politicians who manoeuvred himself into a powerful position in opposition to this perceived threat was Benito Mussolini. Increasingly, land owners and industrialists turned to him as the only figure who seemed to be able to resist the threat of socialism. In 1922 a small number of Mussolini's fascists marched on Rome. King Victor Emmanuel III refused to order the army to disperse the marchers, and instead Mussolini was invited to become Prime Minister. During the 1920s and 30s Mussolini turned his following into a cult, using education and propaganda to link his regime to Ancient Rome and Italy's 'glorious' past.

Axis

The name given to the alliance between Germany, Italy and Japan, along with the eastern European countries that fought alongside Germany and Italy during the Second World War.

In 1940 Mussolini took Italy into the Second World War on the side of Germany, looking for an opportunity to enlarge Italy's territory. However, as the tide turned against the **Axis** from 1942, his support ebbed away. In July 1943 the King ordered his arrest. German troops invaded to stop Italy from leaving the war and Mussolini became the ruler of a German-controlled puppet northern state. In 1945 he was captured and shot by partisans.

After the war Italy received $2 billion of aid through the US Marshall Plan, which began her economic recovery from the war. Nationally and politically divisions remained. In June 1946 Italians (including women for the first time) voted for a Republic, though the vote in the south went in favour of keeping the monarchy.

Is Italy a successful, unified country today?

During the writing of this book, Europe generally and Italy in particular has been through several crises. Italy's economic weaknesses were exposed by the world wide downturn and international financial crisis from 2008 onwards. Unemployment in Italy in January 2014 was nearly 13 per cent of the working population, and in June 2014 the rate of unemployment for young people was over 45 per cent. As we might expect, both of these figures are worse in southern Italy, where youth unemployment runs at 60 per cent.

Italy's political system is still held in low regard by many Italians. Silvio Berlusconi, the most electorally successful of Italy's recent politicians, is currently serving a community service order for tax fraud. The shifts in power, coalition and policy that helped Berlusconi stay in power for long periods between 2001 and 2013 could be described as a continuation of the system of *trasformismo* that maintained the ineffective liberal status quo in the years after unification.

The unification of Italy is still not accepted by all 'Italians'. In Sicily a separatist coalition had the largest number of seats in the Sicilian Parliament between 2008 and 2012. In the north, the *Lega Nord* is a popular party with the aim of creating a separate country called 'Padania', with borders similar to those of the northern state which Cavair had hoped to create in 1859. These separatist groups, and others, watched the outcome of the 2014 referendum on Scottish independence with interest, hopeful that a 'yes' vote for independence might encourage more northern Italians to seek independence from the rest of the country. If other European states continue to devolve power, perhaps the Italian regions will start to pick away at the unity of Italy.

Index